FOUNDATIONS OF COACHING
THE TOTAL COACHING MANUAL

DR. JACK WELCH
WITH DAVID BAILIFF

Wasteland Press
www.wastelandpress.net
Shelbyville, KY USA

Foundations of Coaching:
The Total Coaching Manual
by Dr. Jack Welch
with David Bailiff

Copyright © 2020 Dr. Jack Welch
ALL RIGHTS RESERVED

Additional Contributors:
Jason Mayo, Ed.D.
Jimmy Shuck, Ed.D.
Tracy Welch, M.Ed

First Printing – September 2020
ISBN: 978-1-68111-374-6

NO PART OF THIS BOOK MAY BE REPRODUCED IN ANY
FORM, BY PHOTOCOPYING OR BY ANY ELECTRONIC OR
MECHANICAL MEANS, INCLUDING INFORMATION STORAGE
OR RETRIEVAL SYSTEMS, WITHOUT PERMISSION IN
WRITING FROM THE COPYRIGHT OWNER/AUTHOR

Printed in the U.S.A.

0   1   2

ACKNOWLEDGEMENTS

From the bottom of our hearts, we thank you for reading *Foundations of Coaching*. We hope you will benefit from some of our guidance in helping your coaching career. There is no other job more fulfilling than coaching and teaching children and young adults. Coaches are the backbone of our educational system. You are a leader, mentor, and surrogate parent to countless numbers of student-athletes. Never take that responsibility lightly. Many great leaders of our country are being groomed by our coaches. God Bless in your endeavors.

Kindest regards,

Jack Welch
David Bailiff
Jason Mayo
Jimmy Shuck
Tracy Welch

THANKS, FROM JACK

Jack would like to give special thanks to David Bailiff, Dr. Jason Mayo, Dr. Jimmy Shuck, and Tracy Welch for their input, guidance, and support.

In addition, Jack thanks his beautiful wife of forty-two years, high school sweetheart Carol "Suzie" Welch and his sons Joshua and Steven. "My family support gives me energy and motivation. I am very thankful God has blessed me with such a great family. In addition, to my immediate family, I am thankful to have loving parents and brothers. My mother, Melba, and father, Doyle, always encouraged me to reach for the stars. My father now deceased, was a ball of energy. His drive and intellect inspired me to follow my dreams. He would always tell me to not be a wisher but a doer. My mom has the spirit of a champion. She believes her boys can do anything we set our minds to."

I also want to thank my mentor, Don W. Davis. "Don's guidance and teaching methods during my short time underneath his tutelage laid the foundation for my work ethic."

Special thanks to Bill Freeman, Gayle Miller, Sam Sample, Spud Aldridge, Jerry Jones, Reverend Marshall Stanton, Dr. Dick Hedges, Dick Parker, Dr. Glen Acker, Dr. Rose Cameron, and Blake Powell.

Lastly, thanks to Payton Pardee for pushing me forward in writing this book. "You are headed for the big time; I will be glad to say I knew you when."

Jack Welch

PREFACE

The purpose of *Foundations of Coaching* is to help prepare future and current coaches for all coaching demands. Educated and professionally trained coaches are in great demand! This book provides an in depth look into all areas of coaching required for success. Informed current and future coaches will become innovative pioneers in this niche discipline.

"Having served as a college and high school athletic director for 27 years, it is obvious coaches are not receiving the details of the coaching profession with their degrees. This manual gives insight into the legal aspects of coaching along with things they are about to experience: care and treatment of equipment, budgeting, parent and player meetings, facility maintenance, demands of head coaches and athletic directors, etc." Jack Welch

"As a long-time head collegiate coach, I understand the need for coaches to be prepared for all aspects of the coaching profession. Having a college degree and even playing the sport does not prepare coaches for having to deal with family concerns, player problems, the demands of taking classes, and playing the game. I want to give coaches some key ingredients and insight to all the different aspects of the profession." David Bailiff

The information provided in this manual equips participants with the skills and knowledge necessary to pass state and national certification tests successfully. *Foundations of Coaching* places a distinct focus on empowering coaches with comprehensive knowledge of state and national coaching practices.

Coaching services are integral to all sports and sport related fields, as well as in business professions. Numerous corporations and privately-owned businesses have invested in coaching as a cost-effective way to help employees increase effectiveness, think more creatively, take on greater responsibility, and grow professionally. When coaching techniques and philosophies are employed in the workplace, they create better performing organizations and loyal workforces. Consequently, businesses and school districts are increasingly turning to the skills of coaching for help in developing and implementing career and life plans.

Foundations of Coaching provides a depth of knowledge to excel in this competitive field. Successful sports organizations begin with foundational studies. Current and future coaches will build knowledge in specific areas, such as societal sport, sport administration, sport events and facility management, sport marketing, sport law, and sport economics.

In addition to training in administering and coaching individual sport(s), *Foundations of Coaching* includes sport psychology, sport leadership, and sport communication.

Participants approach this book from multiple roles with a focus on the following:

Designed for School Districts

School administrators and coaches are expected to fulfill requirements of law to ensure students take part in a healthy and respectful environment. One of the important legal responsibilities for school administrators is to select, train, and prepare future teacher-coaches. Training must relate to coaching in an educational setting, which requires different and more complex skills than those for coaching a club team or community program. The United States is the only major country offering interscholastic sports as an extracurricular activity to over 7.8 million students who participate annually.

Design for Business

Simply put, coaching is about enhancing a person's awareness and behavior to maximize their effectiveness through synergy. People who are trained in the art of coaching know their goal is to meet objectives of organizations through a team approach. This includes a healthy understanding of when the good of the team outweighs short-term personal desires of the individual. Skills developed through coaching serve businesses well. The ability to problem-solve, work with others cooperatively, and to motivate people to be their best are all important skills needed in the business field. These are the skills good coaches have. As evidence, notice the high correlation between school administration and coaching.

Coaching in business will address business ethics, global perspectives, and communication. *Foundations of Coaching* benefit both businesses and school districts. Participants gain specific skills integral to the business and educational culture.

Goal Setting

- Certified participants aspire to be managers, looking to implement coaching programs at their own company.
- Certified participants will be career-seekers/changers, looking for a career that helps people reach their highest professional and/or personal potential.

Skills Development

- Certified participants understand their role in organizations.
- Certified participants understand how to build trust.
- Certified participants understand importance and develop capacity to take on roles of internal coaches, looking for additional training to serve their company better.
- Certified participants develop coaching abilities designed to shape a motivational workplace.
- Certified participants understand how to clarify performance expectations.
- Certified participants learn how to give needs-based feedback.

Management

- Certified participants serve as consultants, looking to meet their clients' specific coaching needs.

- Certified participants realize and nurture the talent in others.

Foundations of Coaching prepares current and future coaches in all aspects of coaching. This manual includes University Interscholastic League (UIL) and national coaching certification requirement areas.

Foundations of Coaching awards a certification endorsement. This curriculum trains and educates coaches for fulltime coaching and teaching responsibilities. The career coach/teacher will be prepared for real-life coaching situations. Participants will be current in the ever-changing profession of interscholastic coaching. Whether it be education, law, or medicine, it is vitally important to stay current with best practices, new policies, and equipped to deal with new issues. Coaches need to be current in the areas of teaching methods, risk management communication and motivational skills needed to administer a team or program and to encourage students to be the best they can be in sports and in life.

Program Summary

In summary, this certification program has been designed exclusively to meet the needs of the evolving coaching profession. It provides a structured curriculum covering core principles and practices. It equips future coaches with a necessary toolbox of techniques to become a skilled and confident professional coach in a career, as well as fulfilling a life satisfaction capacity.

Program Outcome

- UIL compliant and certified in required coaching mandates (tackling, hydration, concussions, weightlifting, conditioning, etc.)
- Game management
- Facility management
- Team and player management
- Understand coaching is teaching, and academics come first

Jack Welch, Ed.D. (active), successful career as collegiate and high school athletic director and head football coach.

David Bailiff (active), successful career as NCAA FBS (football bowl subdivision) and FCS (football championship subdivision) head football coach.

Contributors: Dr. Jason Mayo, Dr. Jimmy Shuck, Tracy Welch.

TABLE OF CONTENTS

PREFACE v

COURSE ONE 1

CHAPTER ONE: *Being a Career Coach* 3
   Professional Teacher-Coach 3
   The Role of the Coach is Not Just Coaching! 3
      Role as a Teacher First and Coach Second 4
      Role as the Coach 5
         State Certification 5
         Five Tips for Aspiring Coaches 5
         Join State Coaching Organizations 8
         Athletic Department Philosophy 8
         Staff Support Services 8
         Care for Health and Safety of the Students 9
      Equipment Room Overview 9
         Mission Statement 9
         Organization of Equipment Room 10
            1. Customize Your Storage to Your Needs. 10
            2. Store Paperwork in Mobile Filing Cabinets. 10
            3. Think about Security and Safety. 10
            4. Get Bulky Items Out of Sight. 11
            5. Think About Small Items, too. 11
            6. Make It Easy to Store Players' Equipment. 11
            7. Look for Adaptable Storage Solutions. 11
      Equipment Department Organization 12
         Equipment Procedures (Written in a manual) 12
         Equipment Manager Guidelines 12
            1. Equipment Room. 12
            2. Locker Room(s). 12
            3. Laundry. 13
            4. Game Equipment. 13

  5. Away Game 13

  6. Practice 13

  7. Checklist—Game (Head manager list for all games) 13

 Getting Your Foot in the Door 16

  Entry Level Positions 17

CHAPTER TWO: *The Prepared Coach* 18

 Qualities of a Prepared Coach 18

  Coach Models Positive Behaviors Teaching Young People Valuable Life Lessons 18

  "Change of Mission" for the Athlete. What Happens after a Career Ending Injury? 19

   Be Part of the Team 19

  Promote Learning 19

  Modeling Professional Behavior in All Circumstances 20

  Prepare for Practice 21

   The Practice Plan 24

   Include Weight Room Training 24

  Submit Required Reports to the Athletic Department on Time: Before, During, and After the Season 25

  Communicate Effectively with Students and Parents 25

  Observe and Evaluate Total Sport Program 25

  Community Involvement 26

COURSE TWO 29

CHAPTER THREE: *The Art of Winning and Losing* 31

 The Art of Winning 31

  The Primary Role as a Teacher-Coach 32

  Demonstrate Expertise in All Sports 33

  Teach Best Practices Tactics and Techniques 33

   Understanding Your Passion for the Sport First 33

   Setting the Stage for Teaching 33

   The Importance of "Why" 34

   Fundamentals First, Then Complex 34

   Use the Whole-Part Method 34

   Effective Motivation 34

   The Hoopla of Success 34

   Model What You Preach 35

  Encourage Crossover Athletes 35

 Develop a Winning Culture 35

 Establishing the Student-Athlete 38

 Community Involvement 38

CHAPTER FOUR: *Certification and Legal* 39

 Legal Responsibilities of the Teacher-Coach 39

  Legality and the Certified Coach 40

  Contractual Rights of a Teacher-Coach 42

  The Failure to Warn Theory and Government Immunity (Scope of Duty) 43

  Harvey V. Ouchita Parish School Board 43

  Healthy Lifestyles, Good Citizenship, and Sportsmanship 44

  Life Lessons That Are Not Likely to be Learned in the Classroom 45

  National Federation of State High School Associations (NFHS) Concussion
Management Guidelines 47

   Return to Play Form-Concussion Management Protocol 47

   Immunity Provisions 47

   Requirement for Supervision of the Concussion Management Protocol Program 47

   Concussion Acknowledgement Form 48

  Hydration 48

  Harassment-Sexual 49

  Harassment-Bullying 50

   Physical Bullying 50

   Verbal Bullying 50

   Relationship Bullying 51

  Hazing 51

  Tackling (Training required by UIL and provided by the Texas High School Coaches
Association) 51

  Sharing Coaches and Players with Other Sport Programs 52

  Share Facilities with Other Sports 52

  Discouraging Sport Specialization 53

  Importance of the Weight Room in Training Athletes 54

   Weight Training Athletes Versus Body Building 54

   Strengthening Ligaments and Tendons, While Building Muscle 54

   Proper Techniques of Various Weightlifting Stations: Different Sports Require
Different Lifts 55

COURSE THREE 57

CHAPTER FIVE: *The Head Coach* 59

    The "A" political coach theory: Demonstrating an Understanding of Events Such as But Not Limited To: Black History Month, Veterans Month, Breast Cancer Awareness, National Women's Day, etc. 59

    The Coach Profile: 24/7, 365 Days Representing YOUR School 59

        Developing Positive Relationships: Other Coaches, Administration, Faculty, Community 60

        Developing a Booster Club 60

            Role of Booster Clubs 60

        Handling Finances 61

        Building a Budget 64

            Creating a Budget 64

        Having Athletic Committees 67

        Administration of a Program 68

        Staff Assignments 68

        Staff Meetings 69

            Weekly Meetings 69

        Student Managers 70

        Equipment Duties 70

            Laundry 71

            Example Equipment Organization 71

            Daily Equipment Operations 71

        Training Rules 72

        Physical Examinations and Insurance 74

        Conditioning and Early Practices 74

            Early Fall Training–Conditioning 75

            Conditioning During a Season 76

        Game and Practice Film 76

        Team Meetings 76

        Conflict Management 77

CHAPTER SIX: *Leading the Way* 78

    Game Planning 78

        Game Plan Preparation 78

            Monday 79

            Tuesday–Wednesday 79

Thursday	79
Friday	79
Saturday	79
Film Breakdown	79
The Offense	80
The Defense	80
Special Teams	81
Strategies	81
Proficiency of Technology of Sport	82
Analysis/Quality Control	82
Hiring Practices	82
Leadership of the Head Coach	82
Recommended Books on Leadership: Good to Great and Developing the Moral Component of Authentic Leadership	82
COURSE FOUR	**91**
CHAPTER SEVEN: *The Athletic Director*	**93**
Role and Responsibilities	93
Improve Internal and External Communication	95
Goals and Objectives	96
Professional Standards of Conduct	96
Code of Ethics	97
Relationships with Student-Athletes	98
Policies, Rules, and Expectations	99
Academic Eligibility	100
Accidents and Injuries	100
Athletic Equipment and Uniforms	100
Attendance	101
Communicable Disease	101
Confidentiality	101
Discipline	102
Fire Drill/Emergency Plan	102
First Aid and Medical Treatment	102
Handling Bodily Fluids	103
Handling of "Sharps"	104

       Medications 104

       Insurance 104

       Lightning Standard 104

       Non-Discrimination 105

       Hazing 105

       Parent Meeting 105

       Fundraising 106

       Physical and Health Questionnaire 106

       Political Freedom 106

       Reporting Child Abuse and Neglect 106

       Season Summary 106

       Team Events 107

       Tobacco, Vaping, and Substance Abuse 107

       Training Rules 108

       Transportation 108

       Transporting Students 108

       Travel and Away Games 108

       Unlawful Harassment 108

       Volunteers 109

       Weapons and Fireworks 109

       Training Requirements 109

       Abiding by District Policies 109

   Align and Organize Athletic Department 110

       Conduct Pre-Season and Post-Season Evaluations 110

       Athletic Director and Head Coach Evaluation(s) 111

CHAPTER EIGHT: *Moving Forward* 125

   Support Athletics Mission, Be A Team Member, and Serve Assigned Athletic Duties for the Program: Committees, Sport Assignments, Organizing Sport Spirit Projects/Groups 125

     Develop a Youth Spirit Group: Bleacher Creatures 125

     Promote Importance of Coaches in the Classroom. Add Stipends 126

     Develop Student-Athletes 128

     Assist All Head Coaches in Developing Leaders 129

       1. Performance Leaders (Competition Captains) 129

       2. Locker Room Leaders (Culture Captains) 129

       3. Social Leaders (Chemistry Captains) 129

    4. Organizational Leaders (Campus Captains) 129

    5. Reserve Leaders (Sub Captains) 129

Promote Academic Importance of Athletic Programs 129

Improve Coaches' Abilities and Skills Through Professional Development and
Continuous Improvement 130

Engage Community Stakeholders 130

Facility Awareness 130

    Example of Strategic Planning 133

Strategic Planning: Pulling the Staff Together for "One Vision" 134

    Work the Plan 134

    Have a Date for Completion 134

    Follow-Up on the Project 134

Example of Developing an Athletic Hall of Fame 134

    Guidelines for Nomination and Election 134

        Purpose 134

        Details. 135

Board Members 136

    Election Process 136

    Induction Ceremony 136

Fundraising: What is Fundraising? The Art of Fundraising. Different Fundraising
Methods. Proper Use of Funds Raised 136

    The Art of Fundraising 137

Marketing 138

    Concept of a Good Marketing Plan 138

Guiding the Program in New Directions and Supporting ALL Sports and Athletic Staff.. 140

REFERENCES 143

DR. JACK WELCH 148

DAVID BAILIFF 150

DR. JASON MAYO 153

DR. JIMMY SHUCK 154

TRACY WELCH 155

COURSE
ONE

CHAPTER ONE:
Being a Career Coach

Note: *Foundations of Coaching* is designed for all sports. The authors use examples of football with most illustrations, but these illustrations easily can be used for other sports.

Professional Teacher-Coach

Coaching is a rewarding profession. *My father-in-law, Reverend R. B. Shoemaker, said a coach would impact more people in a week than he would as a pastor in a year. I believe most coaches would agree.* (J. Welch)

How does a person get started in coaching? Former athletes have a clear path but students who did not play the sport(s) wonder how they can break into the coaching profession.

There are several thoughts about coaching interscholastic sports. One theme of thought is to coach a sport as a sideline to the teaching profession. This thought is to simply coach after school to pick up some extra salary. In contrast, a career coach is a dedicated professional. Of course, they are a dedicated classroom teacher as well, but their train of thought is as a professional. Coaching is a way of life. This type of coach is a fulltime coach. They want to compete at a high level.

The Role of the Coach is Not Just Coaching!

1. Sport coaches assist athletes in developing their full potential. They are responsible for
   - training athletes in a sport by analyzing their performances,
   - instructing in relevant skills,
   - providing encouragement, and
   - responsible for the guidance of the athlete in life and their chosen sport.

2. The role of the coach will be many and varied:
   - Instructor
   - Assessor
   - Friend
   - Mentor
   - Facilitator
   - Chauffeur
   - Demonstrator
   - Adviser
   - Supporter
   - Fact finder
   - Motivator

- Counselor
- Organizer
- Planner
- Fountain of all knowledge

Role as a Teacher First and Coach Second

Junior high and high school coaches motivate, instruct, and coach athletes. Their primary responsibility is improving the performance of athletes and building teams to compete interscholastically.

Coaches typically work in teaching positions. Their pay structure is as a teacher first. They receive a stipend for coaching. Teacher duties come first. A coach will work additional hours during the sport season. Many sports such as football, require a work week over 40 hours. Working nights, holidays, evenings, and weekends are common ground for high school coaches. Additionally, several different sport coaches are required to work over Christmas and spring breaks. Many of the sports have summer requirements. A high school coach must be prepared to work in all different kinds of weather conditions. They must also be willing to travel with the team to different locations for games. Coaches run the risk of injury due to the nature of the sport.

Dual contracts are utilized in many states to assure coaches are teachers first and to make sure all coaching duties are adhered to. To receive a contract for an additional year both duties of teaching and coaching must be completed in satisfactory evaluations.

Misconceptions about coaches and the coaching profession arise usually because of past demonstrations of non-professional coaches. A professional coach understands *teaching is coaching*. They are prepared for classroom duties just like they are for their sport. There are many educational values of competitive athletics. Athletics provides opportunities for character development. Being a participant in a well-organized and sound program helps in development of sociological concepts of understanding competition; leadership; self-discipline; respect for authority, man-kind, and gender, race, color, or creed; and sportsmanship to name only a partial list.

Athletes learn about concepts of life and how attitude makes a difference. Attitudes and behavioral patterns are reflected in how an athlete responds in life matters. Pressures from parents, siblings, relatives, friends, and interested community members usually chart the direction of an athlete. Lack of emotional stability in competitive situations frequently result in ineffective responses.

The coach is in a powerful position to help an athlete grow in all aspects of his or her life. Behavior patterns can change. A coach teaches athletes proper behavior characteristics. The adolescent learns by a coach's example and guidance. For a coach to have any carry over of his training in an athlete's life, he or she must teach for it to happen. The teachings should focus on basic problems and solutions to those problems. Athletic experience with quality coaches serves as a guide to living a quality and productive life. Most participants will not play sports after high school graduation. The educational values of athletics must be of the highest caliber. Coaches need to possess skilled human relationship knowledge and sport psychology tactics. The task of coaching, leading, and guiding students in educational life is their greatest call of duty.

Role as the Coach

In relation to sports, the role of the coach is to create the right conditions for learning to happen and find ways of motivating athletes. Most athletes are highly motivated and therefore, the task is to maintain motivation and generate excitement and enthusiasm.

The coach will need to be able to:

- Assist athletes to prepare training programs
- Communicate effectively with athletes
- Assist athletes to develop new skills
- Use evaluation tests to monitor training progress
- Predict performance

Therefore, one can see that it is an exceedingly difficult task and requires a very special person. A coach is always teaching in some capacity.

According to the U.S. Bureau of Labor Statistics, coaches employed with local schools need to meet state certification requirements (*www.bls.gov*). A coach must be trained in CPR (cardiopulmonary resuscitation) and take part in any necessary training or education programs required by the state. If an examination or other requirements need to be completed, then a coach completes them prior to starting their duties. Schools generally work with their coaches to get them certified with state requirements.

State Certification

A high school coach must be familiar with the rules and regulations of the sports they plan on coaching. This is acquired through playing and studying the sport. There are no specific education requirements for high school coaches, but many possess a bachelor's degree in sports science, exercise, kinesiology, fitness, physical education, or physiology. Additionally, many teachers work as high school coaches in part-time positions. If a high school coach goes this route, they also must meet the necessary requirements to be employed as a high school teacher.

Five Tips for Aspiring Coaches

1. **Get Started**

   Many aspiring coaches want to start at the varsity level. This is next to impossible to do. Most teacher-coaches begin at sub-varsity levels. Whether it is junior high school or at the high school level, beginning coaches have a lot to learn before jumping into varsity competition. One cardinal sin is for an inexperienced coach to believe they are ready for an assignment without having the necessary skills to avoid downfalls. Whether it is knowledge of the sport or understanding legal and other various and sundry details of handling parents and players, an inexperienced person can get in way over their head.

"I encourage an aspiring coach to begin in the junior high. These kids want to learn and are green. Their parents do not understand the demands of organized sports. This is the age where coaches must learn to work with both the player and parents, teaching them to be on time, be prepared, and everything that goes along with the sport." (Tracy Welch, Athletic Director, Lake Worth Independent School District)

"You have to be ready to start at the lowest level of interscholastic sports. It is important to learn the tools of the trade. Dealing with parents and players is an important piece to learn. How to schedule parent and team meetings, setting up rules and sport guidelines, handling equipment and facilities are important pieces to understanding what it takes to be a coach." (Rodney Southern, Athletic Director, Huntsville Independent School District)

There are many needs for a community's youth program. *Foundations of Coaching* focuses on interscholastic levels (junior and senior high schools). Recreation programs are especially important and are a learning ground, but they do not have the technical pieces of a school setting.

"I encourage inexperienced coaches to begin at the junior high levels where they are able to make mistakes and learn. Be a sponge and soak up all the knowledge available. Visit high school practices. Go to workshops and clinics. Read books on coaching and ask questions." (David Bailiff)

2. Have a Mentor

Learn from the best. It is important to understand a coach will mimic their mentor. Mentors are valuable and can help guide an inexperienced coach to becoming a great coach. Have you ever heard the saying "birds of a feather flock together?" The same holds true in the coaching profession. Learn from the best. Try to search for a beginning job in a school district known for excellence. What you learn in the first 3 years of coaching will stick with you for the rest of your career. Try to shadow your mentor, whether it is a head coach or an assistant coach. Do what you can to be in their shadow.

This is the time to learn. Make a notebook and keep it for years. Finding the right person to learn from is extremely important. Make sure players are their main concern, not wins and championships. Make sure your mentor(s) are ethical. They do not break rules and display unprofessional behavior. Learn from a person that treats other coaches and players with respect.

3. Have a Vision

What is your purpose? Write it down. Know what it is that you are trying to accomplish. After you write down your vision, then devise a plan. This is to be included in your notebook that I mentioned. Have steps to your plan. Coaching is teaching and great coaches know the path they are on. They know what they are trying to do. The scoreboard is a by-product of what you are doing. If what you are doing is correct and meaningful then the results will follow, showing you are heading in the right direction. If it does not seem to be working, then change paths.

Know what you want to accomplish. Set goals and have a practice schedule allowing the system to flow.

Have a vision, develop a plan, then work the plan. If you do not have a vision and plan, then you are simply taking a walk. Walk with purpose. Know where you are going. Develop your vision and plan from top to bottom. By having a quality mentor, these steps will be much easier because you are learning from an experienced person. Make sure the mentor is the type of person you can respect and tell people about.

"Have a vision and plan. Work your plan to perfection. Coach for the right reasons. Do not focus on yourself and your career but on helping others and molding young people." (Dr. Jimmy Shuck, Principal and former coach, Copperas Cove I.S.D.)

4. Learn, Learn, Learn

Keep your notebook handy. Carry it with you to seminars, coaching meetings, and to the study room. Understand it takes experience to get where you desire to go in your coaching career. It might seem like you are not going anywhere. It might take years to move up. Great coaches cannot be hidden. They stick out. They shine. If you treat players, parents and other coaches by the golden rule and you are knowledgeable about your sport, you will rise through the ranks. A popular sports speaker, Colonel Flowers, said it takes knowledge, confidence, and enthusiasm to be at the height of success (J. C. Flowers, personal communication, June 17, 2020). He is often heard on FM 104.9 "The Horn" as a guest co-host for the *B&E Show*—Austin's most listened to sports talk show. He hosts his own radio show, *The Zero 900 Show*, Saturday's 9-10 am (streamed live at HornFM.com).

Think about that. You need to learn. Develop the knowledge of your sport. Knowledge gives confidence. Having the confidence to share with other coaches and confidence in leading players. Then have enthusiasm. Coaching is fun. Your desire to go to work will be evident. Your desire to not go to work will also be evident. An enthusiastic person radiates excitement. Knowledge gives confidence. Enthusiasm gives excitement. Put those qualities together and you have a winner. Legendary UCLA basketball coach John Wooden once said, "When you're through learning, you're through" (Quoteswise.com, n.d., para. 8).

5. Know Your Why

Have an open mind. Learning is a process. You should never stop learning, even if you reach your highest goal in coaching. If you ever get to the point of not desiring to learn, then I recommend you retire. You build a great career by seeking knowledge and continuing to learn.

Coaching is not all fun and games. Coaches will be attacked, blamed, and cussed. Over the years, coaches will have scars reminding them of their journey. Be prepared to get attacked in the media. Social media carries kibitzers (criticizers).

Some parents and players want their voice to be heard. Some will lobby for a coach to be removed. Rumors will swirl. Usually rumors will be about immorality or finances. Rumors are used to hurt a coach's reputation. A coach should expect falsehoods to be said about them. Coaching is rewarding but a coach needs to have armor of ethics, morality, and honesty on their side to conquer social media rumors and falsehoods.

Being a thick-skinned person will enable a coach to maintain focus. Understanding the world is full of craziness will help keep a coach focused on their vision of helping children succeed. In a future chapter, handling combative and malicious parents and dealing with interference in coaching will be addressed.

Join State Coaching Organizations

Every coach and even future coaches should be members of their state organizations. In Texas, it is the Texas High School Coaches Association (THSCA). Also, become a member of national federations. Being a member will keep you informed of best practices, available clinics, and what is happening in general. Most state organizations have monthly magazines and online notices.

Athletic Department Philosophy

If you are currently a coach, you should have the athletic department philosophy memorized. What is the vision statement? What are the goals of the department?

If you are a future coach, then research a local school district's athletic philosophy, vision statement, and goals of the department. It is especially important and emphasized in this manual; coaches must understand, they work as part of a team. They must know what the team is all about.

Staff Support Services

Services of an athletic trainer, sport manager, student coach, or sport office assistant are considered support staff. What is a support staff person's role in the athletic department? Support staff members work in a wide array of duties. Duties vary from sport to sport. In most instances, they are responsible for routine tasks helping other employees and students with specific tasks. For instance, a student coach might set up practice drills and assist the main coach(es) in operating drills. The training staff assist coaches in injury prevention and rehabilitation. Office assistants assist with bookkeeping, computer duties, and a wide variety of activities.

University Interscholastic League Rules and Regulations

Texas coaches are governed by the UIL rules and regulations. To receive *Foundations of Coaching* star certification, documentation must be presented of visiting an UIL open meeting session. Other state coaches can do the same with their state organization (www.uil.com).

Care for Health and Safety of the Students

Regardless of the age of an athlete, sprains, strains, fractures, and concussions are part of sports. "The Center for Disease Control reports high school sports activity account for more than two million injuries, 500,000 doctor's visits, and 30,000 hospitalizations every year and concussion rates have doubled in the last 10 years" (Garini, 2014, para. 1).

Injuries need to be treated immediately. Quick attention to an injury will have an impact on an athlete's recovery. Many school districts employ certified athletic trainers to handle injuries, but coaches must be educated in the prevention and handling of injuries to keep an athlete safe and minimize the risk of further injury.

It is a coach's responsibility to have information for handling injuries available in a parent manual. With concerns for the health and safety of our young athletes, it is important for parents to understand the education and training of the people working with their athletes and making medical decisions when an injury occurs. Athletic manuals need to include the protocol of handling injuries from the simplest to the complex.

The primary role of coaching student athletes is ensuring students' safety. Teaching the sport and building a team is important, but parents want to make sure their child is safe and secure. Coaches need to think of their student athletes as their children; how would they want their child to be treated? Safety is a must. In this line of thought, equipment used to help keep student athletes safe is crucial and must be in optimal working order.

Equipment Room Overview

Mission Statement

The equipment room role is to promote the growth and well-being of its student-athletes by providing quality, clean, safe, and cutting-edge athletic apparel and equipment for use in practice and competition.

- Equipment Room Goals
    - To provide a safe environment for our student-athletes
    - To properly maintain athletic equipment and apparel on a daily basis
    - Process laundry on a daily basis
    - Be as organized as possible
    - Provide the latest and most advanced equipment

Organization of Equipment Room

An organized equipment room provides documentation of assigned gear daily. Lost and found equipment is properly maintained daily. All equipment is accounted for.

1. **Customize Your Storage to Your Needs.**

    One of the best ways to make the most of your athletic storage space is to start with your goals, and then customize your storage systems to suit them.

    - From lockers for athletes to wheeled carts to transport gear, the storage solutions that are best for your space will be the storage solutions that meet your needs. Ask yourself what your storage space needs to do. What are you keeping there? How are you using it, and how could it be used best? These answers will help you choose the right products and organizational tools for your space.

    - If you have a lot of practice tapes or DVDs on file, invest in media storage cabinets that fit in your space. These will make it easy to locate tapes when you need them while also cutting clutter and wasted space. If you have a lot of paperwork, investigate smart filing cabinets that will tuck away your mountains of player data.

2. **Store Paperwork in Mobile Filing Cabinets.**

    From files about your players to data on the competition, your storage room is likely to be packed with paperwork in no time. But because stacks of papers are hard to sift through, throwing everything on your desk is not going to cut it. Filing cabinets offer an effective solution, but that solution is usually one that takes up a lot of space. That is where smarter options like mobile filing cabinets come in handy.

    - Sometimes called compact storage or movable storage, mobile filing cabinets save floor space by being totally movable, set on wheeled carriages. Rather than needing to arrange your cabinets in permanent aisles, you can arrange them in movable aisles that are easily moved around to create extra space for more productive purposes.

3. **Think about Security and Safety.**

    Because the storage room usually holds expensive equipment and gear, it is important to keep it properly monitored and protected. The right security techniques and products are crucial here, as they will help prevent thefts or break-ins, while also keeping confidential information about players or competitors secure. Consider keyed cabinets or drawers that prevent unauthorized access to private information. Choose storage products that are designed to be hard to tip over or tamper with.

- Products with keypad control offer administrators an even greater ability to manage what is going on in equipment storage areas. Evaluate your options and choose the ones that best suit your space and security needs.

4. **Get Bulky Items Out of Sight.**

    - Nobody must tell you that a lot of athletic gear is bulky, from shoulder pads and helmets to goal posts. Consequently, to manage this equipment effectively, you need a way to tuck things out of sight but keep them easy to access. Whether you opt for shelving or modular casework, you have storage solutions that will organize and streamline your storage space.

5. **Think About Small Items, too.**

    - While a lot of athletic equipment is big and cumbersome, there is also a lot of smaller gear. To keep these items organized, look for drawers and cabinets where you can pack away smaller things. Because there are so many different storage solutions available now, you can easily find drawer organizers and cabinet compartments suited to store everything from balls to chalk to water bottles. What is more, there are locking drawers to protect small items that need to stay secure.

6. **Make It Easy to Store Players' Equipment.**

    - Lockers are the lifeblood of athletic facilities, ideal for storing player equipment and personal belongings. Today's market includes a wide range of lockers in various sizes and styles. You can choose the make, model and number of lockers that work best for your situation, from freestyle personal storage lockers to durable steels lockers made to withstand years of use. Plus, there are all kinds of ways to lay out your lockers to suit your space, making them versatile, useful solutions to athletic storage needs.

7. **Look for Adaptable Storage Solutions.**

    - The ideal storage equipment will be storage equipment that can evolve as you do. When your programming changes and you have different needs, you do not want to have to purchase all new lockers, cabinetry, filing cabinets, and rolling carts. You want versatile equipment that can adapt with you well into the future, equipment that can hold up to years of use and that can serve more than one potential purpose.

The equipment room is to be maintained in pristine condition. Doing so provides a professional appearance, demonstrating the mirror in which the football program is viewed by prospective student-athletes (for college recruiting), as well as the entire football program.

Equipment Department Organization

Equipment Procedures (Written in a manual)

- Equipment Room (players or coaches do not come in if not needed)
- Field Equipment Storage-Outdoor Shed
- Field Equipment (practice/games)
- Laundry (practice/game)

A. Checkout and Check-in Procedures
   - Mark everything—item issued to players and coaches
   - Log in all equipment issued (documentation)
B. Headsets
C. Film
D. Locker room
   - Locker assignments
   - Cleanliness
   - Locker Checks
   - Showers/Toilets
   - Room disinfectant

Equipment Manager Guidelines

- Coordinator
- Student Coordinator
   - Student Assistants
- (List)

1. **Equipment Room.**

   - Organize storage of equipment
   - Check out/in equipment protocol and filing system
   - Inventory
   - Cleanliness
   - Repair Station/Equipment
     1. Sewing kit
     2. Number press (label all player gear with stick on name-last)
     3. All tools and equipment repair material

2. **Locker Room(s).**

   - Locker check-daily (open part of locker only daily, all locker once per week)
     1. Design locker check daily (make list of lockers not in compliance but fix it)

2. All trash and trash cans checked daily (have maintenance schedule)
3. Check showers/sinks/toilets: Soap, cleanliness (Ensure janitorial services)

3. Laundry.

- Practice gear daily (fully dry)
- Issue one towel per player at equipment door
- Weekend-game laundry

4. Game Equipment.

- Weekly check of pants and jerseys for tears-GET REPAIRED
- Check list for sideline and travel for game
- Sideline Heaters
- Sideline jackets for rain-cold weather
- Hand warmers

5. Away Game.

- Check list
- Take brooms-Clean locker room prior and post-game—"Leave it cleaner than we found it"
- Set up locker room for pre-game dress
- Ensure hot water
- Provide towels
- Fans (2)—Rain games (4)

6. Practice.

- Video
- Sideline-Offense and defense equipment repair
- Clock
- Field equipment
  1. Balls
  2. Chains
  3. Dummies: hand shields, agile, pop ups
  4. Chutes with top
  5. Running ropes
  6. Jugs machine

7. Checklist—Game (Head manager list for all games).

- **Players**
  Explain protocol of checking in equipment at team meeting.

- Helmets
- Shoulder Pads
- Knee Pads
- Thigh Pads
- Girdles
- Gloves
- Socks
- Shoes
- Mouth pieces
- All accessories: shoestrings, helmet visors, helmet screws, chin straps, shoulder pad straps, and all equipment necessities.

- **Coaches**
  - Sideline boards-Marking boards (pens/erases)
  - Headsets
  - Benches arranged
  - Coaching boards-Call boards
  - Coaching gear: shirt, pants, cap, gloves, coat

- **Locker Room**
  - Fans
  - 10 Chairs
  - Towels
  - Hot water
  - Cleaning materials: brooms, vacuum (call ahead of time)—"Leave it cleaner than you found it."
  - Soap for shower

- **Pre-Game Responsibility**
  - Equipment checkout
  - Locker room setup
  - Sideline set up
  - Field set up
  - Receiving kicker balls before returners get to field
  - Defensive monitor (check with coordinator)
  - Offensive monitor (check with coordinator)

- **Post-Game Responsibility**
  - Sideline clear
  - Locker room-soap/towels/clean up after players are finished
  - Check in of equipment
  - Headsets
  - Video equipment

- **Staffing**

The equipment room is staffed by equipment managers. The equipment room staff provides student-athletes with
- Top-notch equipment
- Maintenance and accountability of all equipment to ensure student-athletes perform at the highest level possible

The student managers are assigned specific duties based on availability and interest. They work closely with coaches and athletes of the football team, leading to a unique and rewarding work experience.

Example of staffing large school or college program:

Equipment Assignments/Responsibilities/Facilities

- **Locker Room Facility**
    - Shower area
    - Restroom
    - Trash cans
    - Floor
    - Laundry bins
    - Shoe rack area

- **Equipment Room Facility**
    - Washer/dryer area
    - Film table
    - Manager desk
    - Back storage room
    - Roller storage area

- **Clothing**
    - Practice gear
    - Game gear (jersey/pants/socks)
    - Travel suits
    - Shoes
    - Helmets
    - Shoulder pads
    - Coaches gear

- **Students**
    - Prefer to have one student assigned to each position coach (a coach in charge of coaching a specific position group)
    - Two for handling equipment inside and outside
    - Depending on size of team (platoon), three to handle film duties
    - One for period and clock

Getting Your Foot in the Door

Seeing big college games on television, with all the glitter and flash, along with high salaries is how many beginning coaches dream of their coaching careers. In today's world of enormous salaries given to head coaches and high-profile assistants, beginning coaches do not have the reality of what it takes to start in the coaching profession. Many of these high-priced coaches began their careers as the lowest coach on the totem pole. Many volunteered and did not receive any pay for the first year or two. High salaries have drawn a lot of people to the coaching profession. Getting your foot in the door to a lucrative coaching position is extremely difficult for beginning coaches.

To break into a coaching position in college can take years of work, research, patience, and persistence. Just as in any line of work or career field, getting your foot in the door is not all about what you know but who you know.

In many instances in college coaching, once you get your foot in the door, it takes time to work your way to top positions. How do young coaches get into college coaching? There is no standard method or way to get your foot in the door. As previously mentioned, it is usually by who you know, or you have been a successful high school coach. Many quality assistant high school coaches will receive a graduate assistant position. This allows them to get their master's degree and begin a college coaching career.

Salary in high school coaching is based on a pay scale authorized by the school board. Head coaches and athletic directors are usually negotiable. In college, the same holds true for athletic directors and head coaches but the staff is usually at the discretion of the head coach. This is based on the money the college allots for staff. The head coach will decide how each coach is valued and expense the total allotment. When considering being a college coach, you should have the mindset of doing it for the love of the game, not the money. If a person begins in high school it is usually difficult for them to take a college job, unless it is with the bigger classification of colleges, because high schools usually pay much more.

Many coaches in college have at some time or another coached for free, just to get their foot in the door. Many of these coaches start out volunteering. The thing to remember, is regardless of how much you are paid, you do the job to the best of your ability. Regardless if you are working for free, for $10,000, for $100,000 or more, do the job better than anyone else. If you choose to go the route of coaching for free, the job still needs to be accomplished as if you are a top paid employee. People with this attitude will someday be the highest paid coaches on a staff. Your passion and enthusiasm as an entry level coach needs to be the same as a coach making a million dollars.

Always remember this quote from Don Davis (former West Texas State University Athletic Director/Head Football Coach), "It is not the job that makes the man, it is the man that makes the job." He would explain that great coaches would never be paid what they are worth. His advice was to always do a job so well, your boss knew you were under paid.

Entry Level Positions

As mentioned, most coaches get into coaching at the sub-varsity or what is referred to as entry-level positions. The number of sub-varsity positions at each school differs and depends on the size of the school's budget. Most school districts begin sport activities in the junior high, seventh and eighth grades. In college these entry-level positions are sometimes called Director of the Sport Operations, Film Coordinator, and Director of Player Development. In building relationships with other coaches, they need to learn they can trust you.

My first job in college coaching was at a small Division I university, West Texas State University, as a part-time coach. In 6-months working for the university football program, I was paid zero, zilch, "notta," nothing! I had never worked so hard in all my life. My mentor and supervisor was Don Davis. I learned, regardless of my pay, I was given an opportunity to learn and coach college sports. It was a great opportunity. I focused on the job and not the money. I could not have worked in that position if I did not have a supportive family to help me. My supportive family was my beautiful wife. Her small salary for working a fulltime job made it affordable for me to work for free. After 6 months, I was offered an athletic director and head football coaching position in high school. I was the youngest in those positions in Texas at the age of 23. After 2 years, my mentor—Don Davis—was elevated to the head position at West Texas State University and hired me as a fulltime coach. All because of my work ethic and attitude. Most of the time, working in entry level positions, regardless of the salary, pays off. It is who you know that moves you forward most of the time.

Sam Sample, Jack Welch, Don W. Davis

CHAPTER TWO:
The Prepared Coach

Qualities of a Prepared Coach

There are many qualities of a prepared coach. Prepared coaches can be great coaches. Some of these qualities involve being positive, enthusiastic, supportive, trusting, an excellent communicator, vision focused, goal-oriented, sport knowledgeable, observant, respectful, patient and a genuinely caring person.

How do we identify a great coach? What personal qualities do they possess? What separates a great coach from a good coach? Is it training, coaching technique, or instinct? How does coaching knowledge differ from application? Does a great coach have a caring attitude for helping people? Can becoming a great coach be learned or is it something someone instinctively already has?

There is no one single talent a great coach possesses. Great coaches encompass many attributes. They possess a deep love for the game and in helping people. They know how to get results and get the job done. They are tireless workers.

Here is a list devised by David Bailiff, Jason Mayo, Jimmy Shuck, and me. Having combined over 140 years in coaching and education, we have trained many teachers and coaches. We have served as master teachers and mentors to many coaches over the years. Below are the top five qualities we feel distinguish good from great coaches:

- The great coaches were dedicated to learning all aspects of coaching.
- The great coaches had high personal standards.
- The great coaches were tireless workers.
- The great coaches genuinely cared for others.
- The great coaches had respect for others and for the thoughts and ideas of others and were tenacious workers.

Great coaches study continuously. They study other ideas and philosophies. They study coaching techniques and seek out other views. Good coaches have many good traits. A great coach has them all. If you want to be great, then you need to work on all these traits. Being a great coach is not easy but nothing great ever comes easy. Working at developing these traits is the key to becoming a great coach. Evaluate yourself by devising an evaluation sheet and having players and colleagues fill it out anonymously for your review.

Coach Models Positive Behaviors Teaching Young People Valuable Life Lessons

Young people mimic their coaches. Coaches are role models. Great coaches genuinely question, listen, and build rapport with student-athletes and colleagues. Great coaches coach players and coaching is different from training. Although training is a part of developing athletes, coaching is helping the athlete learn and not just training them to be robots.

"Helping student-athletes learn rather than lecturing them" (Dr. Jimmy Shuck, Principal and former coach, Copperas Cove I.S.D., 2020).

"A coach guides, teaches, and helps student-athletes maximize their potential" (Jason Mayo, High School Principal, Temple I.S.D., 2020).

"Change of Mission" for the Athlete. What Happens after a Career Ending Injury?

What does the player do when they have a career ending injury? Are they devastated because they can no longer participate? Are they able to use the lifelong lessons learned from their coaches?

The process of coping with an injury is hard. Here is a list that can help student-athletes to "change their mission" (J. C. Flowers, personal communication, June 17, 2020).

Be Part of the Team

- Attend practices
- Work at the games
- Be a student manager
- Be a student-coach
- Be a student-trainer
- Attend team functions

Stay connected with your teammates. Being a part of the team refocuses the effort of injured players to helping the team in other ways. The injured player needs to be part of the team environment. Teammates are a family. Whether playing or helping, everyone is a part of a unique atmosphere. Being affiliated with your team allows all members to experience the camaraderie connected with a team environment.

Promote Learning

There are many ways to promote learning with your players. To promote learning basically means to have your players be active learners. This means the players engage with the information being taught and having active participation in class or meetings. By working and collaborating, the learner is doing more than listening, they are analyzing subject matter as they demonstrate its value. Relate learning to real life situations.

Lecturing is sometimes necessary but should be utilized as an ice breaker to disseminate information. The goal is to have players teach each other. This a cognitive way of ingesting information. To be able to apply the information engages learners. Whether it is discussion, reviewing application, or practice. Traditional teaching styles are quite different. In traditional styles of teaching, players sit in a meeting (class) room and listen to a coach and not have any input to the content. Basically, the learner is absorbing the information but is not demonstrating they understand.

Learners must be active in the teaching-learning process. *Foundations of Coaching* model encourages active learning strategies. Have discussion time in meetings. Add problem solving in the curriculum and incorporate time for critical analysis exercises. These are some great ways to engage the learners.

Other ways to engage learners include:

- Create ways to engage learners with independent thinking.
- Be creative in engaging learners.
- Allow for critical thinking with learners.
- Have learners collaborate in small groups.
- Have learners invest in the learning model by allowing suggestions.
- Find ways to motivate learners.
- Evaluate classroom performance.

Modeling Professional Behavior in All Circumstances

Modeling professional behavior is a must in education. Today, social media has access to a coach's every move. It is necessary for coaches to understand they are an example to their players and co-workers 24/7. Here are some key components we feel are necessary for coaches to model.

- **Compassion**–Have empathy for others. Respond to players and family members demonstrating care and respect.
- **Grooming**–Be a model for cleanliness. Personal hygiene is a must for coaches. Model a clean, neat, and well-groomed appearance.
- **Integrity**–Integrity allows people to trust you. Trust you with property, confidential information, and learning activities.
- **Knowledge**–Demonstrate knowledge when called upon or the time is necessary to present. Do not be a know-it-all but understand when the right time is to deliver. Do not act like you know something if you do not. It is better to not say anything and let people think you do not know something than to speak and show you do not know something.
- **Respect**–Demonstrate respect to all players and coaches. Be flexible and open to change. Help resolve problems by listening to all points of view. Place the success of the team above your personal views.
- **Self-motivation**–Be competent in content area. Search for new ways of doing things. Talk to leaders in the field.
- **Team Player**–Be a team player. Be willing to do the dirty jobs. Do what no one else wants to do. Show you are a person that gets the job done.
- **Time Management**–Be prompt. Always be the leader in meetings, practices, and other events. Be first to the event and last to leave. Help pick up if necessary. Stay to ensure everything is accomplished.

Coaches must demonstrate professionalism in their actions.

- This is a must. Even if parents or players get heated and want to meet, do not do it. Have a rule all meetings must be before or after practice at an agreed upon time by both parties. The UIL clearly states playing time will not be discussed in meetings. The UIL manual must be reviewed and followed for what can and not be discussed.

Handling disagreements with students, parents, other coaches, or the athletic department.

- As noted above, set an agreed upon time to discuss issues. All school districts have a grievance policy. Find it. Learn it. Abide by it. It will be a good friend to you in your coaching career.

Prepare for Practice

Coaches must prepare for practice. A plan needs to be written down and posted. Practices should be planned in three areas: special teams, offense, and defense. Considerable consideration should be devoted to a practice schedule.

The entire coaching staff should be involved. How can a position coach teach players what is needed if the coordinator or head coach has not thoroughly reviewed a practice schedule? It is difficult. Time will be maximized when all coaches are on the same plan and understand the plan. Our recommendation is to limit maximum practice times to two hours. During the latter part of week, prior to game time, reduce times. Itemize practice sessions. Have time slots for individual and group drills, special teams, and team time. A written practice program is needed daily for consistency.

Post practices on locker room bulletin boards. Do not surprise players, instead keep them informed and expect maximum effort throughout the practice. Prior to season, scrimmage at least once a week and preferably twice. Of course, the extent and number of scrimmages depends on experience and depth of the players. The less game experience requires more scrimmages. Poorer talent level requires more scrimmage time. If you want to play a game, then you need to learn to play a game. Also, less experienced players might understand drills and playbooks, but everything changes when put to test.

Inside the practice schedule: Half-line drills, 7-on-7 drills, pass rush and protection drills, inside run plays and outside run plays, team pass plays, and team run plays. A variety of team situations segment.

The focus is to be game ready by the end of the week. Each day of the week should have specific areas to practice. A totalization sheet of every play—offensive, defensive, and special teams—should be devised to show how many times players reviewed what will be used during the game.

After each practice, coaches meet to evaluate film of the practice and plan practice for the next day. Added plays and situations will be addressed weekly, keeping a chart of everything presented to the team. Do not expect to perform plays or know details of the game if they are not covered in practice. For example: All practices leading up to the game, a coach called for the field goal unit to practice. During the first game of the season, the team scored, and the extra-point unit ran on the field to kick the extra point. There was one player missing and everyone was screaming for the PAT (point after touchdown) team. The coach had to call time out to discover which player did not go on the field. When the coach called on the player and asked him why he was not on the field the player said he only practiced on the field goal unit, not the PAT unit. Well, we know both are one and the same, but this player did not know. Do not take anything for granted.

There should be a base schedule to follow including the addition of new plays and the elimination of unwanted plays. Stay on schedule to allow time for post-practice meetings with players and coaching staff. Make sure to include time for family and social.

Practices should have a time system utilizing a clock or clock management. For example, have a horn in the end zone or in a tower. Have the horn programmed or manned to sound each period of practice. I recommend having practice divided in five-minute periods.

Keep the start time, practice time, and finish time consistent for the needs of each week. Example: Mondays should include a scouting time for the opponent. Tuesday and Wednesdays are the bulk of the preparation for the offense and defense to prepare for the Friday night game. Thursday is a review of all units. Saturdays should be a time to watch the game field, lift weights, and loosen up. Rest on Sundays-no practice. Coaches, athletes, and managers will be confused if the schedule is not consistent. If the schedule time changes, be sure to notify your staff, players, and your managers, especially the equipment manager or your helpers on the field.

Example practice schedule.

10 minutes–Stretch
10 minutes–Individual Drills-Offense
10 minutes–Group Drills-Offense
10 minutes–7-on-7/Pass Protection-Offense
10 minutes–Team-Offense
15 minutes–Special Team Units for the day
- Monday–Punt and Punt Return
- Tuesday–Kick Off and Kick Return
- Wednesday–Punt (Work on fakes) and Punt Block (Work on fakes)
- Thursday–On-side Kick Off, Hands team for Kick Off Return
- Saturday–Walk through corrections for each unit

10 minutes–Individual Drills-Offense
10 minutes–Group Drills-Offense
10 minutes–7-on-7/Pass Protection Offense
10 minutes–Team Defense
5 minutes-Field Goal/PAT and Field Goal Block
110 Minutes

Dual Offense/Defense Practice Schedule

Date		Uniform Helmets Field Stadium		Practice #1			Countable Hours			
Training Room Opens: 6:00 AM		Position		Team			Practice- 120 minutes	Meeting- 30 minutes	120 minutes	
Walk-Through 6:50 AM (10 minutes)		Pre-Practice 7:25 am (5 minutes)		Specialists			Weight Room during class 0			
Period	DRILL	OL	TE	RB	WR	QB	DRILL	DL	LB	S	CB	Period
1	Stretch	Team Stretch					Stretch	Team Stretch				1
2	Stretch	Team Stretch					Stretch	Team Stretch				2
3	Group	LUA DRILL						Pursuit				3
4												4
5	Group	BPU VS. SELF						Ladders/Gets offs	Stance and Starts	FOOTWORK	BP, SF, TW	5
6								Line Drill	Stance and Starts/In-Out zone		T PLANT PROG./TR	6
7	Circuit	FUNDAMENTAL SYSTEM						Sleds	In-Out Zone	COLLISION - BUZZ	W DRILL	7
8	Individual	STANCES	STANCE	Frames	Stance/Start	Frames		E- Stab, T-Hands	High Hat/Low Hat		PAT-N-GO	8
9	Individual	PAD LEVEL/ BAGS	ZONE STEPS/ SHAVES	Ropes	Hand Fights	CLAP	Individual	E- Hips, T-Inside	Spot Drops	MOF DROPS		9
10				Ball Security	Releases	GUN DROPS		Box Drill				10
11	Group	HUDDLE PROC ON AIR (1 HUDDLE SHOTGUNNED)						Formation Recognition				11
12												12
Break	Break	TV TIMEOUT					TV	TV TIMEOUT				
13	Pass Skel	3 SETS	PASS SKELL - Team vs. Defense (1st & 10) (21 Plays/2 Huddles - Tracking Tempo) (Towards the Band Hall)				Pass Skel	4 Corner	7 on 7 (1st & 10) (21 Plays/2 Huddles - Tracking Tempo)			13
14		TREE						Pop Ups				14
15		DBL PUNCH						Hands				15
Break	Break	TV TIMEOUT					TV	TV TIMEOUT				
16	Team	O VS. D (1ST &10 / 15 Plays / 2 Huddles Opposite Directions) (Tracking Tempo) (Groups 1 & 2 Towards McDonalds)					Team	O VS. D (1ST &10 /15 Plays / 2 Huddles Opposite Directions) (Tracking Tempo)				16
17	Team						Team					17
18	Team	Team					Team	T				18
19	FG/FG Block	FG						FG Block				
Word of the Day:											
Meritocracy		A social system or organization in which people reach positions of power based on their abilities									

Consider:

- Conditioning on Monday and Tuesday
- Team Drives on Wednesday (Game Plan in action)
- Game scenarios each day for 5-10 minutes
- Large teams may platoon and practice offense and defense separately doubling the practice time. If so, we recommend shorting the length of total practice time.

Once a season has started, eliminate full scrimmages. Limit to team drives, team pass, or run drills. No more 20 minutes per day, twice in the early weekdays (Tuesday and Wednesday for high school and Wednesday and Thursday for college). High schools should consider a walk through or no practice on Thursday prior to a Friday game and colleges the same on Friday for Saturday games.

Coaches must believe in the practice plan. Their belief radiates to the players. Be prepared for every drill and segment of the schedule. Have extra helpers (student-managers) to assist coaches in setting up drills, preparing equipment, and cleaning up the drill area. NEVER allow equipment to be laying on the field or within the area of actual practice when it is not being used. Accidents will happen. Players will step on a football, someone's helmet, a ball bag, or a variety of items. How senseless this type of injury would be? The plan must prepare the offense, defense, and special teams. Many coaches do not take special teams as important. Special teams are a third of the game and I have won numerous games because of having prepared special team units. Special teams MAKE the difference. If you want great special teams play your best players.

When coaches believe in practice plans, they will be prompt and eager to work the plans. They consistently put emphasis on the need of staying on time with their players as a position coach.

The Practice Plan

Practice plans for Monday, Tuesday, Wednesday, and Thursday are completed on Saturday or Sunday—before coaches go home—by the staff. I prefer to get all the work done, if possible, on Saturday so coaches can have Sunday for family, church, and resting. After each practice session during the week, coaches complete and record additional needs and emphasis for the next day. A checklist of needed items for each unit should be examined daily.

Consequently, each day will have a rough draft. All four days—Monday, Tuesday, Wednesday, and Thursday—will have a rough draft plan but will be finalized the night before each practice. The head coach and coordinators will meet to finish the plan. The offensive, defensive, and special team coordinators will review the plan with the position coaches.

Include Weight Room Training

Weight training and conditioning is also addressed in Chapter 8.

Weight room schedules are vital to having a strong and injury-reduced team for a season. This is an area (much like special teams) where great coaches get an edge on their opponents. How many times do we hear how good a team could have been except their best players were injured? Injuries occur many times because of the body not being prepared. Football is a violent sport and bodies must be ready for contact. Many coaches schedule the weight room after practice. I prefer the weight schedule to be prior to practice, preferably in the morning before school, if practice is after school and opposite if practice is before school. To get 100% effort physically or mentally in the weight room and on the field, bodies must have time to recuperate.

Submit Required Reports to the Athletic Department on Time: Before, During, and After the Season

As a coach, you want players to be on time. This shows interest, respect, and desire. The same holds true for you as a coach. Have assignments completed and turned in on time. Demonstrate you can be relied on and you get the job done. It is better to be early than late. Throughout my years as a head coach, I would rather have a coach I had to pull down out of the stars than poke them in the butt to get them out of a chair. DO NOT be a procrastinator. On the other hand, if it is necessary to ask for more time, do so because uncompleted work is not acceptable.

Work with deadlines MUST be turned in by their due date.

Communicate Effectively with Students and Parents

Having quality parent relationships requires two-way communication. Take the first step. Reach out to meet each player's parent(s). Let them know the rules and expectations by reviewing the parent-player manual. Have a team parent meeting prior to the season.

- Develop an enforceable parent/coach communication policy.
  Distribute a manual and require each parents' signature as receipt of the manual, prior to the season. This will solve almost any problem imaginable. When parents say they do not understand or never knew of a rule or procedure, you can resort back to their signature verifying they were in receipt of the manual. This is the same manual you reviewed in the parent meeting. Without a signed form in the athletic office, I would not allow a player to begin practice.
- Conduct a preseason meeting with students and parents.
  The parent-player meeting can be together or separate. I prefer both. Have a parent-player meeting and a player meeting. Thoroughly review the rules and procedures. Before a player can start practice, a signature from both the parent and player must be on file. This eliminates miscommunication.

Observe and Evaluate Total Sport Program

Junior high school programs should be in line with the high school program. I always want head coaches at the high school level to be involved in the hiring of junior high school coaches. The program at the junior high should mirror the high school program to ensure best practices and successful high school teams. Head high school coaches should be involved in the evaluation of the junior high programs.

State associations are exploring many ways to increase junior high athletics. Athletics is another way of connecting students to the school. Involved, interested students have higher test scores, higher grades, less discipline problems, and lower dropout rates (Lesley, 2010).

Middle schools are involving sixth grade participation because of reasons stated above. Sixth grade exposes students to lessons and skills acquired through education-based athletics. Community-based sports and club teams, where specialization and burnout have increased are not as effective as interscholastic sports with certified coaches.

Authors of this manual understand how middle school and junior high programs work. These programs feed high school sport programs with motivated and prepared student-athletes. Our goal is not to produce world champion middle school stars. Our goal is to prepare young people with certified teacher-coaches who understand the value in teaching an entire child. This is the age to expose all children to sports. This is not the time for specialization but to give the youngster an awareness of multiple sport programs. This will provide a knowledgeable, stronger, and more educated high school student.

Community Involvement

Coaches and business executives are remarkably similar. *When I was started coaching in a small community, my father told me about the importance of joining local civic organizations (J. Welch). He explained leaders of communities are in these clubs and this was one of the best ways to get to know community leaders. Plus, it was a way to show support to the community and not just care for yourself. He was right. I learned in my very first year as the youngest athletic director and head football coach in Texas at age 23 how important it was.*

Being a part of the community provided exposure and opened lines of communication. They were a tight knit group and I was a part of them (J. Welch). They knew what I needed as a coach and understood the program obstacles we were facing. This program had dropped football the prior season because these obstacles were too large to overcome. Consequently, they knew my every step to rebuild this program. They watched and were concerned. They wanted me to succeed.

The first season game finally came. We were playing a team I did not think was particularly good (J. Welch). I told my wife if this team defeated us, we probably would not win a game because I felt they were the worst team on our schedule. The game was on our home field and the stadium was full. People were excited to see what kind of product we were putting on the field. Since I was involved in the only civic organization in town, everyone was familiar with our coaching staff and players. The crowd was excited. Our opponent beat us 47-18. I felt horrible. Saturday morning as I headed to the office, I saw the numbers 18 in every store window on main street. What were these people doing? Were they trying to embarrass me? Were they making fun of us on our loss? I walked in one of the main stores. Stoney Jackson said, "Hey coach, how are you this morning." I asked why all the stores had our score of 18 on their store front windows. I said, "Mr. Jackson, our kids played their hearts out and we did our best." He said the entire community was so proud of us. The community store owners all agreed to get together on Saturday morning and highlight the great game we played by showing off how many points we scored. He told me I probably did not understand the impact we were making. "Coach, you guys scored more points in one game than the team did the entire year before they dropped the sport." He went on and on about the throwback pass, our team scored on kickoff return unit after the opponent kicked off to us after their last score.

I learned in the very beginning of my career; how important local support was to a program (J. Welch). If you get involved with the community, then you will develop a loyal fan base. Of course, it is a two-way street. In exchange for support, your program must be willing to give back. A basic approach is to use your events for food or toy donations. Other ways include helping elderly folks with yard care, clean-up, and a variety of other projects. Consider outreach efforts to local elementary schools, Boys and Girls Clubs, and nursing homes. Most communities have beautification efforts. Visit with the city manager or recreation director.

Community service is valuable on several levels. Being engaged in the community builds loyal fan support and it also demonstrates your commitment to the community as well. How about a community-wide picnic to celebrate the arrival of a sport season? Or how about players staying on the field or court after a game to play with the youth of the community? Youth camps and clinics are also excellent ways to interact with the community.

Engage other students and faculty on campus. Your program will derive substantial support from students and faculty just because you have become a part of their world. With college programs, there is great benefit derived by involving fraternities and sororities. Let faculty know you appreciate their patience with the players and invite them to come to a contest free.

This kind of community service is a win-win for your program. It gains great support for you and your program. It also involves your students with the community which will help those students in so many other ways besides playing sports.

COURSE
TWO

CHAPTER THREE:
The Art of Winning and Losing

The Art of Winning

Great coaches understand how to win with dignity and lose with class. The "Art of Winning" always has potential to fail. Winning is not glorious unless there is potential to fail. Look at coaches fired each year because their team did not win the championship. That organization only values championships and does not understand there is more than winning it all. Challenges leading to success are not real challenges unless they might also lead to failure.

A great coach understands winning and losing is part of the game. If losing does not hurt, then you are probably destined to lose more than you win. Winners win. They think like winners, they work hard and smart, they are prepared, they have a vision, and the list goes on and on. The fact is they will lose some games. What will they do then? How will they react? Their reaction will tell a lot about their character.

In 1994, I started coaching at Copperas Cove High School (J. Welch). The school district was in the largest classification in Texas. This school district was next to Fort Hood, Texas. Fort Hood is the largest military installation in the free world. This little town had grown from a six-man district to the largest district classification in just 30 years. The previous 20 years, the district was 59-185-1 for a 20% win-percentage. Their win-loss record was horrible. Coaches lasted on average less than 3 years.

The first year we took over the program was awesome. Our team had a winning record (5-3-1). The district had only one winning season in the previous 30 years. During the first homecoming of our tenure, we played traditional power Temple High School under the direction of one of the best coaches in the state, Bob McQueen. They were 42-point favorites to win the game.

We were prepared and played a tremendous game. The Wildcats had beat the Bulldawgs just a few years prior by 70 points, so they probably took us lightly. The game was a battle and in the fourth quarter the score was tied 0-0. We lined up for a field goal and the Wildcats blocked it, only to see our boys pick up the blocked kicked on the other side of the 50 yard line and make a miraculous run down the sideline for a touchdown. The score was the only one in the game and we won. This was probably the biggest upset in the state if not the nation.

After the game, I witnessed the greatest sign of character ever in my career. Coach McQueen started running toward me in the tradition of coaches shaking hands after the game. He did not shake my hand though. He ran up to me, threw his arms around me, and gave me a hug. He told me how proud he was of me, our team, and assistant coaches. He told me that was the greatest effort he had ever witnessed by a Copperas Cove team. He said he was proud of us and for us. Now for the rest of the story. Do not think Coach McQueen was pleased because he was not. He and his coaches went back to Temple after the game and worked all night on the film. The practices were very intense the next week for his team. He took this experience and used it to strengthen his team. They went on to win the district and play in the state playoffs.

A few years later, Coach McQueen retired. When our team was preparing for the state championship, I asked him to speak to our team as we were in final preparations. He graciously did. After hearing him speak. I could understand why his teams performed so well. He is a tremendous motivator. By his example he is the type of coach, young coaches need to emulate. He is a champion.

I was the head coach at Copperas Cove for 24 years, finishing with a record of 193-84-1 and two state championship appearances. I have always tried to be like a Bob McQueen when my team was defeated, especially if we were favored to win (J. Welch).

Players and coaches should be held to high expectations. This environment along with holding them accountable prepares them to be successful. The mentality and approach to every workout, team meeting, and practice are important factors to winning. When the team loses though, how will you respond? Many times, coaches assign blame to those attributes, coaches, or players when we lose. Those are not always the reasons teams lose. It just might be possible, the other team was better, had more talent, or received the breaks. The bottom line is losing happens sooner or later. Respond like a champion.

Everyone sees your reaction, especially your players and coaches. I want to be around people that I trust. The integrity and trust among players are essential to winning. It is hard to measure the total impact, but players who do not trust each other do not fully commit to one another. Teams with trust lay it on the line for one another. A team of players having integrity and trusting for one another have a better chance to be great.

The Primary Role as a Teacher-Coach

Coaches are teachers. Many times, when getting into the coaching profession, coaches do not focus on their classroom duties. This is a cardinal sin. Their pay is from the teaching role. Their coaching efforts receive a stipend (extra pay for an assigned duty). Teaching students is the primary focus of a teacher-coach.

I took pride as an athletic director emphasizing to our coaches that I expected them to be the best teachers in the schoolhouse. This has not always been the impression of administrators and other teachers because they would view a lackadaisical effort from many coaches in the classroom. On my staff, this ole dog does not hunt. This means I would not tolerate a coach being a sub-par teacher (J. Welch).

Some teachers give up their time to coach a sport or academic event. They usually receive a stipend on top of their yearly salary for extra duty. This is the reason most coaches are on a dual contract. A dual contract gives multiple assignments to employees. The employee must satisfy both requirements to retain their position.

Demonstrate Expertise in All Sports

This manual is focused mainly on football coaching but is utilized for all sports. *Foundations of Coaching* is aimed at teaching the importance for a coach to be well rounded. It is important to be able to share athletes and facilities. To do that properly, you must understand every sport's needs and necessities. We thoroughly believe coaches having had experiences coaching other sports for their second and third sports will be more understanding and beneficial to an athletic department. Everything from budgeting, staffing, meeting the needs of players and coaches, to time demands can be learned by either coaching or observing other sports.

One of the things I liked to do with my coaching staffs for professional development was observe other coaches in another sport (J. Welch). *When we observe another program, we had a list of things we were looking for such as but not limited to: coaching demeanor, student discipline, assistant coaches' involvement and expertise, hustle, timing, practice organization, and many more.*

I liked to choose coaches in other sports that were successful. One staff I liked to choose was our girls basketball program led by Skip Townsend. Skip's teams were extraordinarily successful. One year they were ranked 2nd in the nation. He went on to have multiple state championship teams at Brock and Argyle. He is now the head coach at Ranger Junior College. If you want to learn how to coach and be the best, then observe the best (J. Welch).

Teach Best Practices Tactics and Techniques

Productive coaches spend 75% of their time teaching the sport to their players, and the other 25% of the time coaching. With younger athletes, this gap increases with teaching becoming more important. The problem is that many coaches do not understand how to teach athletics effectively. Plus, some coaches do not take the time to grasp how athletes learn. Here are nine proven steps to becoming a better teacher and a better coach.

Understanding Your Passion for the Sport First

Before jumping into coaching, first understand your passion for the game. Having a high level of passion for the sport tremendously influences your energy, creativity, and ability to motivate players. Passion is contagious. If one player or one assistant coach comes to practice excited and fired up, that emotion and passion easily is passed to every other member of the team.

Setting the Stage for Teaching

Prior to the first practice, meet with your athletes and explain your role as a coach and teacher of the game. Let them know your purpose is to help improve their athletic skills. Impress upon them that you care about them as people, and you are concerned about their lives even beyond athletics. Feeling cared about makes a player more coachable. Their effort and concentration will increase. If you care enough about them, they will walk through walls for you.

Part of you caring is to work through players' mistakes. Tell them mistakes are part of the learning process, and the only true mistakes are ones of lack of effort or concentration—both of which easily are corrected.

The Importance of "Why"

Do not assume players know why you are asking them to practice a certain technique or to perform a skill drill. Explain how everything has a positive effect on their ability to play. Be as detailed as possible because it is important that they understand why you are doing certain things.

Fundamentals First, Then Complex

Know the fundamentals of the sport you teach. This enables you to design practices for your players' appropriate skill levels. It also becomes easier to assist an athlete who cannot perform a certain skill. After grasping the fundamentals, players move on to practice drills focusing on more than one skill at a time. Do not expect to teach complex skills to players who have not mastered the basics.

Use the Whole-Part Method

Oftentimes, it is necessary to teach skills in parts or steps. Once again, in-depth knowledge of fundamentals gives you an advantage. Teaching a skill in part keeps the player motivated, because they are forming a mental checklist for performing the skill correctly. Educators refer to this as "task-analysis" (Lynch, 2019, para. 1). Task analysis is the process of breaking down a skill or process into smaller steps and sequences.

Moving from one step to the next puts the focus on progress, which allows you to praise the player for grasping a skill and working with the player in areas that need more practice. A good barometer to know if a player is mastering a certain skill is to see if that player is teaching the skill to another teammate.

Effective Motivation

Find something positive to say to every athlete at every practice. This satisfies the athlete's need for attention, recognition, and appreciation. Be specific with your praise, specific praise is used to reinforce the *why* of practice. Always attempt to find more positives than negatives while constantly praising effort.

The Hoopla of Success

When an athlete or team finally masters a skill or concept, do not hesitate to momentarily stop practice to recognize the achievement. Praise their effort and remind your players why mastery of the skill is so critical.

Model What You Preach

Most coaches talk to players about certain values and characteristics they hope to see in all team members. Coaches really are the best positive role models for these values. When stressing good sportsmanship, talk about coaching with honor, respect for the game, and attitude toward officials. When stressing tenacity, never give up. When stressing organization, conduct structured practices. Players look for guidance, so be consistent with your decisions and actions.

Encourage Crossover Athletes

Coaches who are overzealous sometimes encourage their athletes to play one sport on a year-round basis. This can lead to overuse injuries and burnout. Participating in other sports improves the way the athletes play your sport. The movements and skills required for many sports are similar. Consider the footwork necessary for soccer and basketball. They are almost identical.

Productive coaching is highly dependent on the coach's ability to teach their sport. Teaching is not just blowing a whistle, barking out orders, and heading home after a couple of hours. Being a good teacher takes time, effort, practice, patience, and a passion to make a difference in the lives of your players.

Develop a Winning Culture

Coach Chip Kelly said, "culture will beat scheme every day" (Mosher, 2015, para. 2). Culture is something created by a head coach and staff. It is probably the most important ingredient in building a successful program. It is a topic everyone needs to get a hold of because it will either build your program or it will destroy it. Where you find strong, successful programs, you find a culture supporting this program. A program known for fighting and back talking officials will show up in the action of players and coaches in the community and schoolhouse. It starts with the leadership of the program. What is the head coach like? Is he a self-driven and ethical leader? Or is he an unethical and dishonest person?

Culture is not something that changes overnight. It will take time and lots of effort, but the head coach must ensure their culture is implemented. What exactly is culture? According to Merriam-Webster (n.d.), culture is the "shared attitudes, values, goals, and practices that characterizes an . . . organization" (para. 1b). Welch-Bailiff believes there are four common ingredients of culture in a program. These common ingredients are important in developing a program to your personality. The ingredients include values, action, belief system, and discipline. How does culture develop? Ask yourself why this is the right way, how do we develop the program this way, and what are the steps.

Start with why this is the right way. It is the right way because as the leader you want a program to represent your belief system. You must look yourself in the mirror daily and feel good about what you see. Are you a sell out? Are you only wanting to win games? If you are, then the culture of the program will see chaos. The team will succeed only by talent.

Your why needs to have purpose. Players need to learn their why. A coach knowing why, can help lead players to know their why. A great philosopher once said if you know your why, you can endure anyhow.

Is your program unique? What are the values? Great programs lift weights, work on agility, learn proper technique, study playbooks, and take part in meetings but what is it that shapes culture. It is how these areas are conducted. If the coach is a cheater then the program will act accordingly.

Act. Teach it the right way from the very start, just like a teacher in the classroom. The way a teacher starts off handling a class from the first day will be the direction of the remainder of the semester. Players want to be part of a great program. Great programs have high visibility. Abiding by the rules are a must. Actions in everything you do is a must because everyone will view what is going on. When a player throws their helmet on the sideline, what happens next? If the coach sees the action or does not, the crowd did. If the head coach did not see the action but an assistant coach did, what did they do about? Was the action addressed on the sideline? Did an assistant coach say something to player? If they did then the crowd saw action was taken by the staff. The assistant does not have to fully correct the situation but needs to address it and let the head coach know after the game to get the situation corrected. If this is an action commonly being conducted game after game, then it is obvious what kind of belief system this coaching staff has. If fights are breaking out regularly, and other visible "bad" actions, then again, the culture of the team is known.

What is your belief system? State organizations have rules and regulations. Do the coaches and administration follow these rules and regulations to the "T"? Or do they fudge whenever they can get an edge on their opponent? If they break a rule, do they admit the violation and change their way, or do they sweep it under the rug and continue the path they are on?

It was discovered a school district in Texas was allowing their student-athletes to be in two athletic classes. The state organization strictly prohibits this from taking place. Parents in the community did not think this was allowable and questioned the head coach-athletic director. An answer was given by the coach. The answer did not coincide with how the state organization explained the rule. The parent visited with the coach again and explained what the state organization said when asked about the two athletic period rule. Here is where value in a program can be discovered. Is our program only about winning or doing the right thing in all situations? The state organization supplied the answer, which was school districts cannot allow student-athletes to enroll in two athletic periods. This was presented to the district and the district did not correct the rule violation for that school year. The coach continued to state it was alright to enroll in two athletic periods. Immediately, many parents knowing this rule violation wondered if there were other violations being conducted. The players knowing rules were being broken might lose some respect for the coach.

Contrary to these negative actions, if the players are exemplifying hustle, enthusiasm, and good sportsmanship, the crowd will notice. When a negative situation would occur, which is unusual for this team, the crowd will know that is not the regular actions of this head coach and coaching staff. This describes team discipline. Team discipline is displayed in daily actions.

Slogans reinforce the philosophy of team culture. Players will play hard because of their belief system. Is it about team or self? Teams with a team culture will exemplify this attribute. For culture to be about team, Welch-Bailiff believes love has got to the driving force. Love your brother. Our players play out of this world hard for each other because they love each other. This is developed. What does the coaching staff do to instill this characteristic? Love is the driving force of our culture. Look at the world today and see division. People do not love each other. There is division. Get in a locker room and see what happens when players love each other. The world goes away, and the upcoming battle is the focus in the room. A team loving its members will fight to the bitter end. Both Jack Welch and David Bailiff football teams over their history of coaching have won many games in the fourth quarter. Why? Because the characteristic of their teams is they never quit. This means there is a culture of love.

The values, action, belief system, and discipline are discovered in everything happening with a program. We all have different views on handling situations. There is not one sure way to handle each situation, but how the situations are handled will define your program. How do you want your program to be viewed? After a short time, this will be the legacy you leave behind.

A longtime coach was preparing to retire. This coach had a remarkably successful career. The board and superintendent wanted the coach to retire in a certain way. This superintendent told the coach if he did not retire in this fashion, then his legacy would be tarnished. The coach asked why in the world would his legacy be tarnished? The coach explained he wanted to retire and move on. He did not follow the superintendent and board wishes.

What happened next? Well, there were innuendos and questions of the retirement of this coach planted in the community. Can legacy be tarnished? Legacy is the story of a person's life. It is the things they did, the goals that were accomplished, their failures, and their overall history. Legacy is something a person leaves behind to be remembered by. Legacies are pathways guiding people in decisions with what to do or what not to do. One thing to always remembered is a statement from a prominent school lawyer. This lawyer said,

> Do the right things in all actions. Over the course of your career, you will be attacked. There will be innuendos and rumors. Your legacy and character will tell the story. Do not address falsehoods publicly because people knowing you will know the truth and the people who believe lies without verification will not change their mind even if they hear the truth. Consequently, do the right thing and right will prevail.

Culture needs to be cultivated by every coach on the staff. After only a short period of time, players will follow suit. Successful teams and successful programs are player driven, player led, and player guided. Leadership is a skill and must be learned. Great leadership will be defined in players' actions.

Coaches beginning their careers under ethical, honest, and hard-working coaches will be evident in their careers. When a job on the staff is open, see what the head coach does with recommendations from staff members. Staff members, with great work ethic and impeccable character will be listened to much more than a coach with lesser qualities. If a great coach gives a recommendation, then I would listen. I would question a recommendation coming from a less desirable person. As a coach, make sure you surround yourself with people you are proud to display as your friend.

Culture then is environment. If you desire long term success, then make culture your focal point of the program. A strong and positive culture takes time to build but it can be destroyed overnight. Cultivate it daily.

Establishing the Student-Athlete

Coaching is teaching. Teaching young people about the game of life. Coaches teach players the "how." *How* to play the game. *How* to act. *How* to become a better person. All this takes mental toughness and self-control. Coaches need to focus on the most important ingredient of the educational experience and that is getting to the finish line. Earning and receiving a degree. Then becoming a productive member of society.

To be successful in the classroom, student-athletes need to be focused. What does the coaching staff do to assist student-athletes with focusing on the classroom experience? Coaches want their athletes to be successful.

Start off each semester by introducing all staff members to the athletes. Have position coaches take groups of players to each teacher they will be in class with. Have the student introduce themselves. While the position coach is standing next to them, the players will pledge to pay attention, turn in work, and be prepared for tests. The coach will speak up and tell the teacher he is proud of the players and say to the teacher, "Please let us know if there are any ways to assist you with our players."

Community Involvement

Life outside of sports is what coaches are preparing student-athletes for. Establishing student-athletes in the community takes time. This is an area where student-athletes will discover self-worth. Getting involved with the community develops a sense of self-worth by helping others. Some suggestions are to contact the city recreation department and ask for ideas. Some possibilities include a citywide cleanup project. This helps develop relationships. Have a meeting with the mayor and city manager. Assisting a city wide cleanup sparks the entire city. Media attention will promote the event and it is amazing the city involvement that takes place. The win-win is the city is sparked in getting clean and stadiums will be full of loyal and appreciative fans.

Other community opportunities include volunteering at the local food pantry, helping clean elderly citizens yards, shoveling snow in the winter, and have a city-wide walk to say hi to area citizens. These are just a few of the many ways to be involved in the community. The key is do something. Letting the community know our players and coaches care about them will develop the young people and build friendships.

CHAPTER FOUR:
Certification and Legal

Legal Responsibilities of the Teacher-Coach

Legal responsibilities are usually well-defined in school policy manuals and state organization rules and policy booklets. They usually are a point of emphasis in coaching certification programs. State athletic associations, departments of education, and other government organizations disseminate a range of legal responsibilities for a teacher-coach. These responsibilities protect and maintain safety and well-being of student-athletes and emphasize the educational focus of athletic programs. Mandatory child-abuse reporting is a legal responsibility of all educators.

Court rulings or other legal actions enforce warnings to athletes and parents of the risks associated with a sport. It is a coach's duty to inform student-athletes of the dangers of their sport. Failure to warn student-athletes could place a coach and athletic program at risk.

The National Association for Sport and Physical Education is an excellent source to review and research legalities for coaches (https://www.aasa.org). If a problem arises, coaches will need to have documentation they had proper training and demonstrated expertise in the various areas detailed in the standard of care.

The Coaching Youth Sports website provides a snapshot of legal duties recommended for coaches (http://www.positivesportcoaching.org).

1. Assuring practices and games are held in a safe physical environment.
2. Demonstrate proper knowledge and methods of instruction.
3. Provide safe and appropriate equipment.
4. Ensure athletes are not put in harm's way.
6. Provide adequate supervision of athletes.
7. Provide warnings to parents and athletes of risks inherent in sport participation.
8. Demonstrate knowledge of proper training and conditioning practices.
9. Provide ample and appropriate emergency care.

(*Note*: The NFHS Coaches Association Code of Ethics for interscholastic coaches www.nfhs.org)

1. Enforce training in prevention harassment and discrimination by coaching staff and athletes.
2. Conduct training on how to report suspected child abuse to proper authorities.
3. Family Educational Rights and Privacy Act of 1974 training. Conduct training on respecting and protecting the confidentiality of student records.

4. Conduct training and explain how to report breaches of ethical behavior by colleagues.

These lists are sample guidelines for coaches' legal responsibilities. Coaches also have ethical responsibilities. This is not intended to be a complete list. Coaches must be thorough, check with federal, state, and local guidelines and certifications. Not performing these guidelines will probably not result in criminal charges but could cause a civil judgment to be rendered against you. To achieve the mission and goals of an appropriate interscholastic sports program, coaches should have knowledge and understanding of this information. The goal is to win, but to win the correct way. Never sacrifice character and safety for wins.

Below are the ethical obligations of a coach and athletic program. Learning to be a productive citizen with high character and positive social values is the goal of athletic programs. Coaches have the responsibility to teach and model good citizenship and sportsmanship. Respect for opposing teams and fans, coaches, parents, and officials are at the top of the list.

The mission statement of the athletics program should include a philosophy statement relating to the focus of the community. Achieving the goal of educating student-athletes about the relationships and show concern for the community is reflective of the emphasis of athletic programs. The programs are meant to produce concerned citizens of good character.

What is the goal of athletics in college settings? It is to gain an education, receive a degree, and be a productive member of society. Student-athletes involved in sports must be given attention and time to develop proper skills of sport and life. Programs must care for all players, not the elite few.

Ethical responsibilities of a coach should include but are not limited to:

1. Create a healthy and safe emotional environment.
2. Teach good citizenship and sportsmanship.
3. Respect the other players, coaches, and all affiliated with the sport programs.
4. Assist all players, not just the elite few.
5. Understand and teach life skills, not sport skills only.

Legality and the Certified Coach

Many public-school teacher-coaches in Texas have additional assignments. These assignments include but are not limited to being boys' and girls' sport coaches and other extracurricular activities. What are the rights of coaches regarding a continued expectation of employment? Are these positions guaranteed from year to year? Does the teaching position and coaching position relate to contractual employment or are each separate in nature?

An employee's legal rights as a teacher and coach depend on three different factors:

- The type of contract. Is it probationary, term, or continuing?
- Is the term of service (number of years) covered by the contract?
- Does the contract include specific language as to a specific professional capacity (or capacities)?

A single contract with added duties is different from a dual contract. A single employee contract may appoint them as a teacher. Contracts appointing them as a teacher and a coach is called a dual contract. The single type of contract is the most prevalent today. A single contract provides flexibility for both the employee and the school district. Chapter 21 of the Texas Education Code (2017a) states an employee, employed on a single contract, has a continued expectation of employment as a teacher (absent proper, documented cause for nonrenewal or termination). If this teacher has additional duties added to their assignment, however, such as assigned coaching duties, the employee will not have any legal expectation of continued employment as a coach.

As a teacher with a single contract, coaching duties and corresponding stipend(s) are referenced as a supplemental duty assignment. The supplemental duties clause provides such duties may be terminated at any time by either the teacher or school district at the end of the contract term. Under the single contract, a teacher has no legal right to continued employ as a coach. If relieved of his/her duties under a single contract their only option to contest that action is through the school district's grievance process.

A school district can elect to employ a teacher with coaching duties by issuing a separate written contract. This separate contract is for a term of no more than 1 school year. This option does not provide an employee with any assurance of employment in capacity of coach beyond the given school year. A separate contract for coaching should not be considered with a written notice of employment of additional duty assignment(s) and stipend(s). Normally, Chapter 21 of the Texas Education Code (2017a) does not apply to these contracts.

A dual contract is preferable for a teacher-coach. A school district may elect to employ coaches under a dual professional capacity. This contract is known as a dual contract. This type of contract, authorizes the employee to a legal expectation of continued employment in both positions, teacher and coach, absent properly documented reasons for nonrenewal or termination. Unless employed under a probationary contract, an employee with a dual contract has substantive and procedural due process protections afforded by Chapter 21 of the Texas Education Code (2017a).

On the flip side, under a dual contract, the school district need only have proper cause for nonrenewal or termination of employment in either one of the positions. The dual contract also includes a stipulation an employee may not resign from one position without also resigning from the other. The employee does not have a right for continued employment in a single professional capacity. A coach employed under a dual contract is not entitled to a *specific* coaching assignment, unless specifically stated by the contract.

Although an employee with a teacher/coach contract could request reassignment to a single teacher position and contract, such should be done with the advice and assistance of legal counsel. The school district normally requires an employee with a teacher-coach assignment to sign a dual contract. The teacher has no right to demand a change in professional capacity.

It is important for any employee to review his or her contract carefully before signing. Check the wording. Any change in professional capacity needs to be designated by a corresponding contract. When being issued a new contract, employees have a right to be employed in the same professional capacity. Any questions should be addressed prior to signing the contract.

The following information is provided for general information purposes only. This information is not intended to replace the advice of an attorney.

Contractual Rights of a Teacher-Coach

>A significant case concerning contractual rights of coaches was litigated by TCTA in the mid-1980s. *Hester v. Canadian Independent School District* involved an assistant football and basketball coach employed under a unified [dual] contract. The school district was unhappy with the failure of the high school football team to produce a winning season and qualify for the playoffs and decided nonrenewal for Coach Hester's contract. (Texas Classroom Teachers Association, 2020, para. 13)

>On appeal, the commissioner of education ruled in favor of Hester, thereby overturning the local school board's decision to non-renew his [Hester's] contract. The holding in this case addressed several important points and is still good law today. (para. 14)

>First, the commissioner recognized a school district has the option of employing a coach by either a single capacity ("teacher") contract with supplemental coaching duties or a unified [dual] contract for "teacher/coach." Since Canadian ISD had elected to employ Coach Hester under a unified [dual] contract, nonrenewal required proper cause and documentation of a reason listed in district policy. (para. 15)

>The reason offered by the school district for proposed nonrenewal was "a lack of student progress." However, the district's documentation failed to support this claim, and the teacher evaluation showed Hester had performed well in the classroom. Further, . . .the team had shown improvement not only as to win/loss record, but in other significant ways as well. [The fact was the team did not make the playoffs that fall.] Thus, there was not sufficient evidence of "a significant lack of student progress" to non-renew Coach Hester's contract either as a teacher or as a coach. (para. 16)

The most significant point in the Commissioner of Education's holding was the following:

> [It must be evident] that an athletic team's won-loss record is relevant to an assessment of a coach's performance.... A poor record does not constitute [evidence of] bad coaching.... A win/loss record does not in any way constitute poor coaching. (Texas Classroom Teachers Association, 1985, para. 17)

There are "too many other factors influence a won-loss record" (para. 17). Many of these factors are not controlled by the coach. Example of some these factors include but are not limited to, talent and "ability of his players, the caliber of the opposition, and injuries to key players" (para. 17). The commissioner further stated, "even if it had been appropriate to consider a team's record for assessing the performance of a head coach, extending this analysis to assistant coaches was not justified" (para. 18).

The Failure to Warn Theory and Government Immunity (Scope of Duty)

All coaches are responsible for the safety of their players. The failure to warn theory is about negligence to safety of players (Petraglia et al., 2015). Over the years, situations have been litigated because of injuries sustained during contact sports. Skilled attorneys can innovatively create theories. These theories will have final judgment decided by a jury. Juries are charged with ensuring compliance with how law is interpreted. Coaches should understand the complexities of their sport. Using the head in football is prohibited, but many coaches will praise players for tackles, although the player is using their head to make the tackle. When improper technique is conducted by the player and instruction has not corrected the problem, coaches can be held liable if an injury should occur.

Harvey V. Ouchita Parish School Board

Michael Harvey played football for the West Monroe High School football team in Ouachita Parish, Louisiana, during his sophomore and junior years (Petraglia et al., 2015). Michael established himself as an excellent player. Prior to beginning his senior year, during football practice he suffered two minor neck injuries. Harvey's father was a chiropractor and treated his son for these injuries. He visited with Michael's coach explaining Michael needed to wear a neck roll during all practices and games for an indefinite period of time. He further stated the neck roll was to protect Michael's neck from further injury.

Michael hurt his neck extensively during his senior season (Petraglia et al., 2015). The neck roll was torn off his shoulder pads. It was in such disrepair; it could not be reattached to his shoulder pads. During halftime of the game, Michael requested an extra neck roll. He was informed there were not anymore neck rolls available. Michael returned to play in the third quarter without a neck roll. During a play, Michael made an interception and was tackled by the face mask during the return. He sustained a ruptured disc at C4-5. His injury was severe and permanently damaged him.

As result of injuries sustained on this play, Michael's parents filed suit against his high school football coach and school board (Petraglia et al., 2015). At trial, the court found the coach and staff negligent. The coach and school board failed to require a player to wear available protective equipment to minimize risk being injured when tackled. Although, actions by the opponent violated game rules, judgement was if Michael would have been wearing protective equipment as requested by a doctor, then the injury would have been minimized or never happened. The judgment of the court awarded Michel $215,000. This judgement included $35,000 because he lost an opportunity to play college football. By returning to play without specifically asking the coach for a neck roll, the judgement was to reduce the award by 20% for Michael's portion of his comparative fault.

As a government employee, coaches have what is called "official immunity" (Evans et al., 2019, p. 16). When a person is injured on government property, which a public-school district is government property, then the employee is protected by the law. Texas common law provides for individual immunity from liability. This does not protect them from a lawsuit for negligent acts, as listed above. Government employees exercising their official duties cannot be held liable. This is called "qualified immunity" (p. 13) or official immunity. The Texas Tort Claims Act states government employees are protected when acting in official capacity.

School districts have written policies. District employees are to strictly follow these policies. When an employee acts outside their scope of duty then they can individually be held liable. What is scope of duty? Scope of duty for an employee means performing any duties which a governmental entity requested. This requires or authorizes a public employee to perform regardless of time and place of performance of the requested duties.

For example: School policy specifically says outside entities and patrons must have a written agreement to use school facilities. Coaches traditionally are in control of athletic facilities. A local AAU basketball organization, operated by a prominent community person, asks the athletic director for keys to all the school gyms so the AAU teams will have a place to practice and play games. Without written approval and without a signed facility usage agreement, the coach gave keys to this person.

One evening a group of people were in the gym playing around. A child of the participants was not being supervised. The 3-year-old child climbed up on the bleachers and slipped off. The fall broke the child's neck and resulted in a loss of life. Could the coach, giving out an authorized use of keys, be held liable or does the coach have governmental immunity as described by law for governmental employees? This coach acted outside their scope of duty. They were not authorized to give keys out randomly without a facilities usage agreement. This action was against school policy. The coach can be individually held liable in situations like this.

Coaches make sure you do not give access to school facilities without proper documentation. Always follow school policy.

Healthy Lifestyles, Good Citizenship, and Sportsmanship

Athletic programs need to place an emphasis on healthy lifestyles, good citizenship, and sportsmanship. Playing sports will someday come to an end. Have coaches taught the importance of a healthy lifestyle? Healthy lifestyles are not the sole basis of being healthy but emphasis on having a healthy lifestyle will plant seeds in young people about the importance of being fit. Being healthy means being mentally and emotionally fit. What is a healthy lifestyle? A healthy lifestyle should be part of your overall being. Living a healthy lifestyle helps prevent chronic diseases and long-term illnesses. It is all about feeling good about yourself and having a good quality of life. Athletes must take care of their health. This is important for positive self-esteem and self-image. Maintaining a healthy lifestyle provides a better quality of life for a lifetime.

Citizenship is not the same for everyone. Aside from the legal definition of citizenship, what does it mean to be a good citizen? Most definitions of citizenship identify a range of attributes and actions. Searching definitions and looking at what others have said, we have chosen several attributes to describe citizenship. These attributes include obeying the law, being honest, showing respect, being helpful to others, and being a productive member of society.

Sportsmanship, fairness, respect, and equality are well-known values in athletics. Are these the same values in education? Of course, they should be. As we described earlier with the act of sportsmanship of legendary coach, Bob McQueen, sportsmanship is an act of generous behavior or treatment of others, especially in a sports contest.

Life Lessons That Are Not Likely to be Learned in the Classroom

Education and jobs go hand-in-hand. A good education helps graduates to land good jobs. This is why it is imperative we push for good schools. Good schools are an important part of attracting industries and jobs to a community. Education is in the news constantly. We consistently hear about the need to invest more in reading, math, science, and computer courses. This is understandable but there is more to educating young people.

Participating in sports is an education of its own. There are many educational benefits derived from participating in sports. Notice we said participating, because playing and participating are two different things. Participation can mean being a helper (student-manager), student-trainer, and many other areas of participation. Playing and participation in sports teach many things to young people.

Sports teach important life lessons. The classroom basically teaches subject matter at the higher levels. The higher in education, the more emphasis is on subject matter. If you desire to see teaching in its purest form, view an elementary teacher teaching kindergarten or first grade. When you play sports, you learn about hard work and sacrifice, working together as a team, respecting one another, and having a common goal. Sports teach how to win with pride and lose with dignity. It also teaches how to get up after being knocked down. How to overcome obstacles. How attitude is everything.

Athletics and academics go hand-in-hand. Research continually shows that districts spend on average 3% to 4% of the total budget on extracurricular activities (Milder, 2019). The funding is small for fielding an athletic program in a school district, but the yield is great.

Whether it is salaries, price of new facilities, or equipment needs, the cost of an athletic program in public schools has always been a contentious topic (Milder, 2019). With the public-school finance system in disarray in Texas, it is important for the product to justify the costs. Stanley Laing, Northeast Independent School District's Executive Director for Athletics stated when he was a former high school principal, he witnessed the positive effects athletics made on students' lives both inside and outside of the classroom. He said he researched the district and discovered nearly 40% of students in the NISD district participated in athletics in 7th and 8th grade. In high school, almost 25% of the student population participated in extracurricular activities at the NISD district that included 15 high schools. He further stated NISD attendance rates were 1.7% higher for athletes.

Since state funding dollars are tied to daily attendance rates, one additional percentage point can result in thousands of dollars of additional funding per day. Research clearly shows that students who are in class achieve at a higher rate (Milder, 2019). Laing said NISD student athletes graduated at an astonishing rate of 97.1% and the non-athlete in NISD graduated at a 90.1% rate.

Across the nation, it is well documented, athletes also score higher on standardized tests and have fewer discipline referrals. The benefits of athletics are numerous. Students connected to the schools perform at a much higher rate than students not involved in school activities. I asked a high school principal to research the top 50 academic grade point average students and the bottom 50 grade point average students where I was currently coaching (J. Welch). The data showed the top 50 students had a 94% participation rate and the bottom 50 students had a 98% non-participation rate.

It is important for schools to do everything possible to locate, recruit, and maintain quality teachers and coaches. It is also important to get as many students as possible to be involved in school activities, so they connect to the school. Connecting students to school activities help their academic performance.

These are all important lessons that matter in every work environment. Sports mirror life. Sometime in a sports contest a team receives a bad call from the referee or umpire. What happens next? You can either get bitter (lose the game) or decide to get better (adapt, put the bad call behind, do your best) and win the game. The great coach Sam Sample taught that one letter could be devasting in words: the letter i (focused on oneself) or e (focused on we). When obstacles are confronted, people can choose to be bitter or they can choose to get better. Bitter and better only have one letter different but the meaning of the words is totally different.

Sports teach important lessons about life. Lessons of life applicable in every work environment. There needs to be a good balance of both in our children's lives. Research continually demonstrates extracurricular spending only amounts to a districts' spending on average 3% to 4% of the total budget (Milder, 2019). The funding is small, but the yield is great.

It is important for schools to do everything possible to locate, recruit, and maintain quality teachers and coaches. It is also important to get as many students as possible to be involved in school activities, so they connect to the school. Connecting students to school activities can help their academic performance.

Concussion Protocol (Taken from the UIL [2020b] Rules and Regulation Handbook)

Concussions received by participants in sports activities are an ongoing concern at all levels. Recent interest and research in this area has prompted reevaluations of treatment and management recommendations from the high school to the professional level. Numerous agencies and associations throughout the United States responsible for developing guidelines addressing the management of concussion in high school student-athletes have developed or revised their guidelines for concussion management.

The information provided here will update interested stakeholders on the UIL requirements for concussion management in student-athletes taking part in activities under the jurisdiction of the UIL and will also provide information on compliance with Chapter 38. Subchapter D of the Texas Education Code (2011) that was amended by the passage of House Bill 2038 during the 82nd legislative session.

National Federation of State High School Associations (NFHS) Concussion Management Guidelines

"A concussion is type of traumatic brain injury that impairs normal function of the brain (NFHS, 2017, para. 1). It occurs when the brain is rocked back and forth or twisted inside the skull because of "a blow to the head or body. What may appear to be only a mild jolt or blow to the head or body can result in a concussion" (para. 1).

"The understanding of sports-related concussion" has evolved dramatically in recent years (NFHS, 2017, para. 2). "We now know that young athletes are particularly vulnerable to the effects of a concussion" (para. 2). Please find the following information from the National Federation of State High School Associations (NFHS, 2017).

Return to Play Form-Concussion Management Protocol

This form must be completed and submitted to the athletic trainer or other person (who is not a coach) responsible for compliance with the Return to Play protocol established by the school district Concussion Oversight Team, as determined by the superintendent or their designee (Section 38.157 (c) of the Texas Education Code, 2011).

Immunity Provisions

The Return to Play Guidelines required by state law indicate that parents, in consenting for their student to return to participation following a concussion, understand the immunity provisions contained in the law. Those immunity provisions are contained in Section 38.159 of the Texas Education Code (2011).

Requirement for Supervision of the Concussion Management Protocol Program

Section 38.157 (c) of the Texas Education Code (2011) now requires that, in regard to the Concussion Management Protocol for the school district: "The school district superintendent or the superintendent's designee or, in the case of a home-rule school district or open-enrollment charter school, the person who serves the function of superintendent or that person's designee shall supervise an athletic trainer or other person responsible for compliance with the return-to-play protocol. The person who has supervisory responsibilities under this subsection may not be a coach of an interscholastic athletics team."

For additional information and the specific language contained in the law, please download a copy of H.B. 2038 (2011) as passed by the Legislature and signed by the Governor.

Concussion Acknowledgement Form

The UIL (2012) has created this Concussion Acknowledgement Form, which was required for all student athletes in Grades 7-12 beginning with the 2012-13 school year, because of the passage of HB 2038 from the 2011 legislative session.

According to Section 38.155 of the Texas Education Code (2011), "a student may not participate in an interscholastic athletic activity for a school year until both the student and the student's parent or guardian or another person with legal authority to make medical decisions for the student have signed a form for that school year that acknowledges receiving and reading written information that explains concussion prevention, symptoms, treatment, and oversight and that includes guidelines for safely resuming participation in an athletic activity following a concussion."

Hydration

Athletes must be encouraged to begin exercise well hydrated. Explain to athletes to never be thirsty. This means to continually hydrate. When an athlete is thirsty, they are beginning to be dehydrated. Athletes need to consume enough appropriate fluids during exercise. These fluids should be limited to limit water and salt deficits. Available evidence suggests many athletes begin exercise already dehydrated. They fail to consume enough fluids to counter sweat losses.

It is also important to teach athletes not to consume too much fluid during exercise. Consuming too much water or fluids can cause hyponatremia (Stöppler, 2020). Common sense advice is to help athletes assess their hydration status and develop a personalized hydration strategy. This allows athletes to account for exercise, understand the environment, and know their individual needs. Pre-exercise hydration status can be assessed from urine frequency and volume. There are information charts showing urine color to determine if an athlete is dehydrated or not (Wojcik, 2019).

Change in hydration during exercise can be estimated from the change in their body mass. The sweat rate can be estimated if fluid intake and urinary losses are also measured. Sweat salt losses can be determined by collection and analysis of sweat samples. If athletes are accustomed to losing large amounts of salt, they are likely to be aware of the taste of salt in sweat. Salt crusts on skin and clothing will be evident. Fluids providing electrolytes, should be taken before, during, and after a period of exercise. Strategies will vary greatly between individuals and will also be influenced by environmental conditions, competition regulations, and other factors.

Harassment-Sexual

Every school district and college will have policies about sexual harassment (United Nations, 1992). Coaches must thoroughly understand and teach their team about this important area. Time and time again, coaches and student-athletes find themselves in a jam because of not understanding what sexual harassment is. Students and employees are legally protected against sexual harassment, regardless of the perpetrator's age or status. Although caution is needed when responding to complaints, school leaders should avoid making backroom deals with staff members accused of molestation or improper sexual conduct. All school community members need information and ongoing professional development.

> Unwelcome sexual advances, requests for sexual favors, and other verbal or physical conduct of a sexual nature when:
>
> - Submission to such conduct is made either explicitly or implicitly a term or condition of an individual's employment.
> - Submission to or rejection of such conduct by an individual is used as a basis for employment decisions affecting such individual.
> - Such conduct has the purpose or effect of unreasonably interfering with an individual's work performance or creating an intimidating, hostile, or offensive working environment.
>
> Unwelcome Behavior is the critical word. Unwelcome does not mean "involuntary." A victim may consent or agree to certain conduct and actively participate in it even though it is offensive and objectionable. Therefore, sexual conduct is unwelcome whenever the person subjected to it considers it unwelcome. Whether the person in fact welcomed a request for a date, sex-oriented comment, or joke depends on all the circumstances. (United Nations, 1992, para. 1)

Sexual harassment involves many things including but not limited to:

VERBAL

- Referring to an adult as a girl, hunk, doll, babe, or honey
- Whistling at someone, cat calls
- Making sexual comments about a person's body
- Making sexual comments or innuendos
- Turning work discussions to sexual topics
- Telling sexual jokes or stories
- Asking about sexual fantasies, preferences, or history
- Asking personal questions about social or sexual life
- Making kissing sounds, howling, and smacking lips
- Making sexual comments about a person's clothing, anatomy, or looks
- Repeatedly asking out a person who is not interested
- Telling lies or spreading rumors about a person's personal sex life

NON-VERBAL

- Looking a person up and down (Elevator eyes)
- Staring at someone
- Blocking a person's path
- Following the person
- Giving personal gifts
- Displaying sexually suggestive visuals
- Making sexual gestures with hands or through body movements
- Making facial expressions such as winking, throwing kisses, or licking lips

PHYSICAL

- Giving a massage around the neck or shoulders
- Touching the person's clothing, hair, or body
- Hugging, kissing, patting, or stroking
- Touching or rubbing oneself sexually around another person
- Standing close or brushing up against another person. (United Nations, 1992, para. 2)

Harassment-Bullying

Athletic programs have been in the news over a course of time because of bullying. Bullying in the dressing room or on the field of play is when someone seeks to harm, intimidate, or coerce another person perceived as vulnerable (Texas School Safety Center, 2020). Hazing is a form of bullying and has legal consequences. Bullying can result in assault charges. Whether it is physical of verbal, bullying is causing harm to others.

Bullying is repeated aggressive behavior. It can be physical, verbal, or relational. It can also be in-person or online. Relentless bullying is done repeatedly. It can be for short or long periods of time. If a person is living in constant fear of where and when the bully will strike next, then police and other authorities need to be notified.

Physical Bullying

This type of bullying includes hitting, kicking, or pushing. It can also be threatening. It can include stealing, hiding, or ruining a person's things, and hazing, harassment, or humiliation.

Verbal Bullying

This type of bullying includes name-calling, teasing, taunting, insulting, or otherwise verbally abusing a person.

Relationship Bullying

This type of bullying includes refusing to talk to you, excluding you from groups or activities, spreading lies or rumors about you, making you do things you do not want to do.

Boys usually bully using physical threats and actions. Girls are more likely to engage in verbal or relationship bullying. Either gender can do any of these things. No type of bullying should ever be tolerated.

Cyberbullying utilizes technology (Stopbullying.gov, 2020). This means bullying is no longer limited to schoolyards or street corners. Cyberbullying occurs anywhere, at home, on smartphones, on emails, texts, and social media. Cyberbullying can take place 24 hours a day. Cyberbullies use digital technology to harass, threaten, or humiliate people. Unlike traditional bullying, cyberbullying does not require face-to-face contact. Cyberbullying is not limited to just a handful of witnesses at a time, it can reach limitless amounts of people. It does not require physical power or strength in numbers.

Hazing

Hazing in athletics usually stems from upperclassmen and tradition. It can used for team unity or it can destroy team unity. Regardless of the intention, hazing is unlawful, and coaches and players can get in a lot of trouble for allowing hazing to take place in a program (Jonas, 2017). Hazing is anything done to create humiliating and sometimes dangerous initiation rituals.

At Florida A&M's the Marching 100 members were suspended for hazing rituals causing a death in 2012 (Kunerth & Balona, 2012). The incident resulted in the resignation of the university president and band director. The hazing also caused legal conviction of several band members for felony hazing. This drew the public's attention to intense hazing rituals and ultimately put the perpetrators in prison.

Tackling (Training required by UIL and provided by the Texas High School Coaches Association)

If you are not a current THSCA member and cannot access the ATAVUS tackle training using your THSCA member number, please visit this PDF link for further information from the UIL (2020a) on how to obtain your ATAVUS ID through the UIL Portal via Register My Athlete so you can still complete training online: https://www.uiltexas.org/football/page/atavus-online-procedures-directions-for-tackling-training

All coaches in Texas must have this certification (UIL, 2020a). Tackling techniques have changes drastically over the years and this certification will attest you have been educated in correct tackling procedures. As referenced in *Failure to Warn Theory* section, allowing players to tackle incorrectly can cost the head coach financially. If coaches are coaching and enforcing proper technique, they have government immunity in case of tragic injuries or death. If a player consistently uses their head in tackling and this action has not been corrected, coaches very well can be held liable.

The certification includes introducing concepts every coach should know in order to effectively coach tackling (ATAVUS, 2020). The initial certification will be in person. After completing and passing the certification, coaches will have access to the ATAVUS Digital Coaching Academy. The academy provides coaches access to technical drills, decision-making drills, game-based drills, certification test results, and additional coaching resources to help reinforce the certification process and provide instruction in teaching safer and more effective tackle drills.

Sharing Coaches and Players with Other Sport Programs

Most school districts share assistant coaches. Coaches must coach a variety of sports. Although their main sport might be their love, these are professional educators and they are expected to perform their best in all duties. Very few districts can offer a dual contract to a teacher-coach for single sports. A single-sport coach is usually a teacher recruited to fill a spot. Sharing coaches strengthen athletic programs. It builds unity among staff members and breaks down barriers.

In high school athletics, friction is usually found in boys sports between football and basketball. In girls sports it is usually between volleyball and basketball. Coaches only interested in wins do not care about having multiple sport athletes and multiple sport coaches. This is a shame. Children should be encouraged to play more than one sport, especially if they are capable.

There will always be student-athletes needing a little push to play other sports. Playing multiple sports teaches important skills that can be used in all sports. Other body parts (muscles) will be strengthened. We can all tell stories about a player that should have played another sport but did not. In 1996, I (J. Welch) had a great freshman athlete say he wanted to go straight basketball. In visiting with this player, I discovered basketball was his love, but he was also a great football and track athlete. He was convinced to stay out one more year in football and track to see how he developed. It was important for this athlete to know how much more marketable he would be to college scouts and how much better his body would develop. Well, this young man was the top basketball player for his time in high school. He also was also a stellar athlete in football and track. He received a Division I football offer where he started for 4 consecutive years. He was a second-round draft pick and started in the National Football League (NFL) for 14 consecutive years, earning All-Pro and NFL Man of the Year honors. His name is Charles "Peanut" Tillman.

Share Facilities with Other Sports

Sharing sports facilities gets easier when you become acquainted with your colleagues. Understanding school facilities are for children, then sharing facilities becomes a need for helping sports. Most school districts do not have enough facilities to treat each program like a Division I university, where every sport has an ample amount of facilities. It is imperative each sport works with other sports.

The rule of thumb is the sport in season has priority. For example, during the fall when volleyball is in season, basketball teams must give volleyball the prime time for use of the court. Also, important to note is the sport which utilizes a facility has priority over other sports during the same season frame time. Example, if the weather is not conducive for the football team to practice outside and they do not have an indoor facility to use, then volleyball would have the priority for the gymnasium. Although basketball would normally go next, football is in season and would have second priority.

These things should be discussed in staff meetings, where all coaches know and understand the protocol. Thorough communication helps to eliminate the bevy of minor issues and concerns coming with sharing playing space.

Discouraging Sport Specialization

Specializing in youth and high school sports have become increasingly common. There is a tremendous rise of club and select youth sports programs. These programs operate on a nearly year-round basis. The exact definition of sport specialization varies, but it generally refers to athletes who train intensely in one sport for most of the year at the exclusion of other sports.

> According to a University of Wisconsin study that surveyed more than 1,500 athletes at Wisconsin high schools during the 2015-16 school year, 34% of the athletes specialized in one sport. Another study, presented in 2017 by the American Academy of Orthopaedic Surgeons, found the rate of single-sport specialization among high school athletes to be 45 percent (Van Til, 2019, para. 6).

One of the first questions I (D. Bailiff) ask a high school recruit is how many other sports they participate in. I want to know the other sports he plays. What all does he do in athletics and other school activities? What are the positions he plays? Is he on the basketball, baseball, or track teams? Is he a pitcher, catcher, or outfielder? All of those things are important to me. This shows me their diversity, their ability to play other sports, and it tells a lot about their character.

Sport specialization is a training method. Young athletes hope to achieve stardom. They choose a main sport. Who knows what would have happened if Charles Tillman would have quit all other sports besides basketball?

Several "sports medicine organizations have published recommendations based on the limited evidence available on this topic" (Jayanthi et al., 2019, p. 1040). Documentation shows there are more injuries and less development in sport specialization.

> Injury, overuse injury, serious overuse injury, and lower extremity injury were likely associated with higher degrees of sport specialization in various populations. Sports medicine organizations in general recommended against sport specialization in young athletes and instead promoted multisport participation for physical and psychological benefits. Few long-term data suggest that sport specialization has negative health-related quality-of-life consequences. Higher degrees of sport specialization likely pose risks of overuse injury; however, the age of specialization at which this risk occurs is not known. (p. 1040)

Importance of the Weight Room in Training Athletes

Weight training increases bone mineral density (Mannie, 2014; Westcott, 2012). Strength training places stress on the body, which helps the body to adjust itself. Many positive benefits to muscle and connective tissue takes place when an athlete properly trains with weightlifting. Benefits are numerous but most importantly increased bone density results in stronger bones that are more resilient to injury.

Coaches teaching the importance of weight training have informed players. When athletes understand the importance of a proper strength and conditioning program, they enhance their performance. Weight training for athletes can be general or sport specific. A quality generalized weight training program develops adequate levels of strength. "Strength is a foundational attribute for improving athletic performance" (Meglio, 2011, para. 2). Athletes should focus on developing speed, power and explosiveness. These athletic components are critical to athletic performance.

"Athletes need to work first on increasing relative body strength" (Meglio, 2011, para. 3). Exercises such as "push-ups, pull-ups, hand walking and rope climbing, to name a few" (para. 3) are especially important for an overall body improvement. Athletes handling their own bodyweight will see dramatic improvements in "strength, speed, power, explosiveness, mobility, and other physical attributes" (para. 3).

After mastering the bodyweight of an athlete then there is a need to develop strength in "functional, multi-jointed compound lifts like squats, deadlifts and weighted chin-ups" (Meglio, 2011, para. 4). "Compound lifts" assist athletes in mastering "forceful contractions" (para. 4). This will improve motor skills. "The combination of strength and skill will help athletes reach their maximum potential" (para. 4). The third phase of weight training will focus on building "a solid base of strength" (para. 4). This is when strength coaches will "incorporate speed, power and agility training into their workouts" (para. 4).

Weight Training Athletes Versus Body Building

Weight training prepares athletes for sports and not just muscle building. Muscle building is a by-product of weight training. Athletes run, jump, twist, and turn. Arnold Schwarzenegger won Mr. Universe, but when he started training for his movie career, his weight training changed drastically. No longer did he work on just building muscle. He had to lose weight and train where his body could run, jump, twist, and turn, which are totally different weight training techniques.

Strengthening Ligaments and Tendons, While Building Muscle

This is where understanding how weight training helps an athlete be prepared for competition. An athlete will experience less injuries and be more physically fit to participate in sports when the joints of their body are strengthened. Where are most injuries in a sport? Statistics show injury areas for each sport. Example, a pitcher in baseball needs to have a full range of shoulder use. Using bands to strengthen the shoulder along with dumb bell work is extremely helpful. Knowledgeable coaches understand what different positions on sport teams are needed. The basic thing to remember is weight training should strengthen the joints of the body. What are the joints of the body? There are ligaments and tendons in all joints (shoulders, elbow, ankles, knees, wrists). All weight exercises should be full range and not have too much weight on the bar. Power lifters and body builders wrap the wrist, elbow, and knee joints because the weight they are pressing is too much for the joint to handle. Prevent injuries with your athletes and focus on full-range exercising with amount weights they can handle, only needing a spotter for when they get exhausted. If the spotter is lifting the weight, then there is too much weight on the bar.

Proper Techniques of Various Weightlifting Stations: Different Sports Require Different Lifts

You do not have to be a professional weightlifter or professional athlete to enjoy the benefits of weightlifting. Done properly, weightlifting will help athletes to lose body fat, increase muscle, and provide a healthier body. The key is to learn how to lift properly. Full range and number of lifts per exercise is essential. Professional strength coaches understand the importance of interval training. There is a difference between off-season, pre-season, and in-season training. The rule of thumb is to have 24 lifts per station. Example on the three major body parts (legs, arms, chest), make sure you lift the weight 24 times. This could be three sets of eight or four sets of six. Try to always get that amount of repetitions. On the last lift, if the athlete does not require any spotting to finish the lifts, then the next time they come in to lift, increase the weight by 5 pounds for the exercise (if it was 185 pounds on the bench, then next time start with 190 pounds).

How often should an athlete lift weights? They can lift everyday but DO NOT lift the same body part every day. Give a day in between each body part to lift.

Before athletes start lifting, make sure the weightlifting regimen is tailored for their sport. Cross country runners do not need the same weight training as a football player. A baseball pitcher and basketball player need different weightlifting exercises as well. Girl athletes weight training is a must. Check with manuals, certified strength coaches, watch videos, and countless other means in developing a thorough weight training philosophy for your sport.

COURSE
THREE

CHAPTER FIVE:
The Head Coach

A head coach is a professional at training and developing athletes. They hold a public profile and are remunerated more than other coaches for these additional responsibilities. The head coach position is a miniature schematic of the athletic director position. Many head coaches serve as an athletic director.

The "A" political coach theory: Demonstrating an Understanding of Events Such as But Not Limited To: Black History Month, Veterans Month, Breast Cancer Awareness, National Women's Day, etc.

Head coaches need to be genuinely concerned for all athletes and assistant coaches. All families are affected by the happenings of life. Whether it is a loved one with a fatal disease or a friend, feelings and emotions run rampant with players and these issues need to be addressed.

> Black History Month–Consider addressing this month with a speaker.
>
> Veterans Month–Consider having a veteran speak to the players.
>
> Breast Cancer Awareness–Have a pink out promotion for fans. Have players adorn a piece of clothing or uniform for the game.
>
> National Women's Day and other important days–The school district and community leaders should have a well thought out plan of how the coaches and players will show respect. These are teachable character traits for the players.

The Coach Profile: 24/7, 365 Days Representing YOUR School

- The head coaching position is one of the most premier jobs in any community. It is necessary for head coaches to understand all eyes are on them. They are expected to be leaders in the community and school district. They are responsible for all their actions. People view head coaching as an honorable position.

- Head coaches are expected to deal with situations with integrity and dignity. Their players and assistant coaches are expected to be a replica of their coach. The program is to be organized and function effectively. The head coach is also expected to be a good listener and listen to suggestions.

Developing Positive Relationships: Other Coaches, Administration, Faculty, Community

Good working relationships create benefits: work is enjoyable, productive, and more creative. Team members are more likely to accept changes because trust develops in an atmosphere promoting congeniality. Overall, the program is more innovative and creative.

Good relationships give us freedom. Opportunities become prevalent. The team sees obstacles as a bump in the road instead of an unpassable washed out bridge.

Good relationships perpetuate coaching careers. When people like you, word spreads and vice versa. A very influential community member was telling about meeting the new head football coach at the local Lions Club meeting before the season started. The head coach was giving his speech and afterward was shaking hands with guests. The community person, who was also on the school board, invited the new head coach to his church. Whether the new coach was joking or not, he told the person there was no way he would attend his church because everyone at his church believed if a person did not attend that particular church then they would not be saved. How well do you think this went over in the community? The coach departed the district after only two seasons.

Developing a Booster Club

Role of Booster Clubs

Neighborhood patrons form booster clubs to help enrich the school's participation in extracurricular activities. The fundraising role of booster clubs is particularly crucial in today's economic climate. Positive and direct communication can prevent most problems. Keep the superintendent informed of all activities.

- Have a chain of command for communication with the administration.
- Clear all activities through your administration.
- The superintendent or a designee who does not coach or direct a UIL contest but has approval authority over booster clubs should be invited to all meetings. All meetings should be open to the public.
- Booster clubs should apprise school administrators of all club activities. Make sure your local administration has a copy of all booster club publications. Invite administrators to all booster club meetings. Have an officer meet with the school administration regularly.
- School administration should apprise booster clubs of all school activities.
- Booster clubs do not have authority to direct the duties of a school district employee. The scheduling of contests, rules for participation, methods of earning letters and all other criteria dealing with inter-school programs are under the jurisdiction of the local school administration.
- Minutes should be taken at each meeting and kept on file at the school.
- Periodic financial statements itemizing all receipts and expenditures should be made to the general club membership and kept on file at the school. (UIL, 2020c, para 2)

Handling Finances

Whenever a coach handles money, make sure there is always another person to document the handling of the money. When taking money at games, two people should count the money, place monies in a sealed bag and deposit after the game. Banks have night depositories. NEVER take money home. If the athletic office has a safe, this is allowable. Again, two people must verify the money and deposit or put in the safe together.

Example of procedures for handling athletic funds:

Receiving money for athletic events and other school activities. All personnel responsible for accepting money for games and events must be registered with the Treasury Services office. This person will be given a gray box, numbered tickets, plastic deposit bags, and tracking forms.

Responsibility and duties:

- Receive petty cash money from event administrator. (Amount not to exceed $100.00)
- To accept cash and make change for people entering an event
- Each person is to receive a numbered ticket
- Each ticket is to be tracked and logged accordingly
- At the end of event, the tickets will need to be counted and verified with cash received
- The money needs to be sealed in a clear plastic deposit bag labeled ADMIN from SCHOOL and EVENT NAME.
- The bag needs to be given back to the campus Administrator upon completion.
- The courier service will pick up bags from campus to deliver to Admin/Treasury
- Treasury Services will verify event cash and report any discrepancies. Any person found unable to perform cash handling procedures will be removed from their privileges to collect money for district events.

MORE INFORMATION IN DETAIL IS PROVIDED ON THE FOLLOWING PAGES OF _____ INDEPENDENT SCHOOL DISTRICT.

SUB-VARSITY GATE RECEIPT PROCEDURES

THE FOLLOWING PROCEDURES MUST BE FOLLOWED FOR EVERY EVENT: Before the game:

- Go to the front office of the host school to pick up a locked zipper bag that holds the $100.00.
- You must verify this before using. If there are any discrepancies you must report it to the Treasury Services Office immediately, PHONE NUMBER OF OFFICE RESPONSIBLE.

- Upon receiving the gate change you will need to complete the upper half of the ticket sales report by filling in the Event, (For example: Boys Freshman, Girls JV, Middle School Boys), the Campus where the game is being held, ticket colors, beginning ticket number, and price for each color of ticket being used.
- The lower half of the Ticket Sales Report will list which Sport, Event Date, and Team names that are playing.
- All of this information MUST be filled in correctly, if there are any discrepancies the paperwork will be returned to you for corrections and will then cause a delay in payment for game workers.
- After the game: Finalize the upper half of the Ticket Sales Report by filling in the ending ticket numbers.
- Calculate the total tickets sold for each color and calculate the amount received for each color.
- In the TOTAL CASH line, calculate all the money you have on hand (i.e., the money received plus your gate change), less the gate change line will always be $100.00 and the TOTAL DEPOSIT should always match the TOTAL LINE from the top half of the form.
- Sign your name as the ticket seller with your SCHOOL ID number.
- Also, the Statistician and Timekeeper will need to fill in their names as well for all to get paid.
- Only people working the game should sign the form.
- Referees will give you their own forms to send with your report and ticket stubs. This will ensure that they get paid.
- You must have a ticket stub for every ticket that was sold. DO NOT SHARE YOUR TICKETS! The tickets issued to you are to be sold only by you. The tickets are considered currency and it is your responsibility to return either the ticket stub or the cash equivalent. NO EXCEPTIONS!
- The tickets stubs are to be put in the clear plastic bags with the cash deposit and forms.
- Afterwards you will SEAL the bag and mark on the outside the date, amount of cash and to whom the bag is going.
- The bag will always go back to ADMIN.
- Once you are done the Administrator for that school will come by and pick up your deposit bag and the $100.00 gate change.
- Please make sure the gate change is back in the locked bag and the bag is locked.
- If you only have large bills left please be sure to inform the Administrator.
- The Administrator will lock the bag back in the Vault secure for your next event.
- You are financially responsible for all your supplies (money box and tickets)!! They are always to stay with you and secured when not. If there are any questions, please call: PHONE NUMBER or email PERSON IN CHARGE WITH EMNAIL or email SECOND PERSON.
- Those in attendance at SCHOOL DISTRICT OR COLLEGIATE athletics contests are NOT allowed to leave once they are inside the gate. However, at times it is necessary for adults to leave and then return to a contest. Adults

- WILL be required to show their ticket stubs upon their return. If a ticket stub is not available, they will be required to pay again to re-enter. STUDENTS ARE NOT ALLOWED TO LEAVE A CONTEST ONCE THEY ARE IN ATTENDANCE; this includes students who attend free or on a pass. If a student leaves a contest, they will be required to pay to re-enter.
- ALL DISTRICT OR COLLEGIATE employees will be admitted to all local athletics contests free of charge if they present their identification to the gatekeeper. THIS PASS IS FOR THE EMPLOYEE ONLY and is available to all contests INCLUDING GENERAL ADMISSION AT VARSITY FOOTBALL GAMES.

RECEIPT: I hereby acknowledge receipt of a copy of the (INSTITUTION NAME) Cash Handling Procedures and Policy. I agree to read and abide by the procedures defined and referenced in this document. The information provided in this document is subject to change and changes will be posted in the online version of this document. I understand that changes in District or College policies and procedures may supersede, modify, or eliminate the information summarized in this document. I accept responsibility for reading and abiding by such changes. I also understand that this document is also available on the District's or College's website www.(institutionname).org. I understand that the online version is the most current and authoritative.

I accept responsibility for contacting Treasury Services or the Controller if I shall have any questions or concerns regarding this document. I also understand that by not abiding by such policies and procedures will result in my loss of ability to perform any cash handling duties.

Signature of Employee _____

Date _____ Printed Name _____

Campus/Department _____

- THEFT OF PUBLIC FUNDS IS A FELONY

Building a Budget

The head coach should never go overbudget without the permission of the athletic director. Be thorough and frugal with all budgeting matters. When ordering equipment, make sure school district policy is followed. Prior to ordering equipment, quotes must be secured. The bidding process and purchasing should be conducted by the business office. If the head coach handles this action, make sure all policies are strictly adhered to. Always remember misappropriation of funds is one of top reasons school administrators are relieved of their duties.

Coaches are subject to criticism. Make sure to do everything perfect with handling finances. DO NOT take equipment home or store equipment for the district. All school district items need to remain on campus. Issued coaching clothes and work-related items (Laptops, iPads, etc.) are permissible but tractors, furniture, and other various items must remain on campus.

Example of creating an athletic budget.

Creating a Budget

Every year, athletic directors are responsible for managing athletic department finances. They make important financial decisions. These decisions will impact the institution and programs. To be prudent and fiscally responsible, it is imperative to establish a plan of action for all financial decisions. A detailed budget will be comprehensive and provide a well thought out vision.

Here a few things to think about when creating a budget:

1. What is your vision for your athletic department?
   a. What are your long-term goals?
   b. What are your short-term goals?

2. What are your sources of annual income?

   Some examples might include county allocations, gate receipts, booster club funds, donations, and department fundraising.

3. What are your anticipated annual expenses?

   Some major examples include officials, transportation, equipment and supplies, uniforms, reconditioning, awards, and security.

4. Break down all expenses by team and by gender when possible. This is an important component of any athletic budget to ensure compliance with Title IX (TexasLawHelp.org., 2020).

5. Establish and incorporate an emergency fund into your budget. There are always unanticipated expenses arising over the course of the year.

6. Create a spreadsheet to organize your data and provide an analysis of your income and expenses. Have the Athletic Business Manager, financial assistant, or assistant athletic director if you need assistance with this process.

Here is an example of a budget spreadsheet for different sports and their expenses:

Sport	Officials & Transport	Travel	Travel Meals	Equipment Fees & Record	Uniforms	Equipment	Supplies	Supplies Rentals (Specify)	Facilities Maintenance	Totals
Baseball	$0.00	$0.00	$0.00	$0.00	$0.00	$0.00	$0.00	$0.00	$0.00	$0.00
Basketball	$0.00	$0.00	$0.00	$0.00	$0.00	$0.00	$0.00	$0.00	$0.00	$0.00
Cross Country	$0.00	$0.00	$0.00	$0.00	$0.00	$0.00	$0.00	$0.00	$0.00	$0.00
Football	$0.00	$0.00	$0.00	$0.00	$0.00	$0.00	$0.00	$0.00	$0.00	$0.00
Golf	$0.00	$0.00	$0.00	$0.00	$0.00	$0.00	$0.00	$0.00	$0.00	$0.00
Lacrosse	$0.00	$0.00	$0.00	$0.00	$0.00	$0.00	$0.00	$0.00	$0.00	$0.00
Soccer	$0.00	$0.00	$0.00	$0.00	$0.00	$0.00	$0.00	$0.00	$0.00	$0.00
Softball	$0.00	$0.00	$0.00	$0.00	$0.00	$0.00	$0.00	$0.00	$0.00	$0.00
Swimming & Diving	$0.00	$0.00	$0.00	$0.00	$0.00	$0.00	$0.00	$0.00	$0.00	$0.00
Team Tennis	$0.00	$0.00	$0.00	$0.00	$0.00	$0.00	$0.00	$0.00	$0.00	$0.00
Tennis	$0.00	$0.00	$0.00	$0.00	$0.00	$0.00	$0.00	$0.00	$0.00	$0.00
Track & Field	$0.00	$0.00	$0.00	$0.00	$0.00	$0.00	$0.00	$0.00	$0.00	$0.00
Volleyball	$0.00	$0.00	$0.00	$0.00	$0.00	$0.00	$0.00	$0.00	$0.00	$0.00
Wrestling	$0.00	$0.00	$0.00	$0.00	$0.00	$0.00	$0.00	$0.00	$0.00	$0.00
Total	$0.00	$0.00	$0.00	$0.00	$0.00	$0.00	$0.00	$0.00	$0.00	$0.00

Every athletic budget will include transportation, meals-travel, equipment for the sport, supplies, facility maintenance.

7. Once you have your numbers in place, analyze the following:
   a. Is your allocation of funds in compliance with Title IX?
   b. If you have a shortfall of funds, develop a plan to make up the difference?
   c. If you have a surplus of funds, how will they be used?

8. Previous year's financial figures are crucial to financial planning. For example, when anticipating income from football gate receipts, think about your opponents, the date/time of the games, and plan for some inclement weather. Consider home and away contests. It might be to your benefit to contract with your opponent for the home school to keep all gate receipts, especially if you have good attendance.

   With expenses, be aware of any increases for the upcoming year.

   For example, transportation costs for school system transportation increased 25% this year.

9. Use your fellow athletic directors as a resource. Each school is different, but you can always learn from your colleague's best practices.

10. Include your business manager in the budget process and make sure you have his or her approval each year. Strong financial management is crucial to success as an athletic director. By creating and following a budget for your department, you will go a long way in achieving that success.

Having Athletic Committees

- Team Leadership Council. Have different position players and leaders in this group. Voted on by teammates.
- Student Athletic Advisory Council. This is a group better used by the athletic director but can also serve a head football coach. Since the head football coaching role is probably the top job in the community, have some captains, along with one player from each team on campus, a teacher, and administrator. Review everything within the program. Get their advice, listen, and give information you need relayed in the school and community.
- Parent/Faculty/Community Athletic Advisory Council. I love this committee. Have parents volunteer to be on this committee and also choose a faculty member, administrator, and a few community members. This will be your eyes and ears of the community. On my committee, I was blessed to have our mayor, a city council person, district attorney, business leaders, and some parents.

Administration of a Program

Sport programs require efficiency to ensure success. Administration of a program takes organization and constant evaluation. Deputization and supervision are important concerns. At the large high school and collegiate ranks, many head coaches' main duties are in the realm of administration. With increased pressure on winning, organizations becomes more meticulous. Administrative planning is of paramount importance. An extreme amount of time during in-season and off-season is devoted to careful planning. The more preseason effort will help lesson season administrative demands.

Duties of coaches in relation to individual and team play, strategy, and scouting are all necessities of a head coach. This chapter will focus on duties related to staffing, training rules, conditioning, practice and game plans, game statistics, visual motivations and teaching devices, and team meetings.

Staff Assignments

Coaching staffs are composed of assistant coaches and scouts. Many of these coaches are sub-varsity coaches: junior high, freshmen, or junior varsity. Staff personnel are chosen for skill and experience. There will be a head coach, assistant head coach, coordinators, and assistants. At the junior high levels, there will usually be a school coordinator as well. The number of assistant coaches usually depends on the size of school and the number of teams.

Using football as an example, it is the task of the head coach to synchronize coaches into a team. Explicit assignments will be assigned to each coach, including duties off the field as well as coaching position duties. I have always said better coaches are people who get things done without griping and being pushed to do more. I have always included a poem about service.

I slept and dreamt life was joy. I awoke and saw that life was service. I acted and behold, service was joy. (Rabindranath Tagore)

Assistant coaches help prepare daily schedules. Their input is valuable. They are responsible for individual drill work necessary for game plan preparation. Assistants must maintain the philosophy of the head coach and coordinators. Never should assistant coaches improvise or change procedures without authority to do so. I believe assistant coaches are recommenders.

Coordinators should build the offense, defense, and special teams play book with total cooperation of assistant coaches. All play books should match what the head coach desires. After putting the books together, then a total review with the head coach is necessary. Example: There are multiple ways to run the sweep. It can be a swing sweep, a downhill sweep, a sweep off tackle, or a sweep outside the end. If any coach or player does not do what the entire unit is supposed to do, then failure is destined. All final decisions should be agreed to by the head coach. Head coaches will listen to opinions, weigh the merit of the suggestions but will make the final decision. When it is fourth and one in punting territory, there can be recommendations, but there is only one decision maker—the head coach or designee.

Coaching staffs are families and need to remember what goes on in a family stays within the family. There will be differences of opinions. There will be differing philosophies, but it is critically necessary for all staff members to understand, the head coach answers for everything within the program.

Staff Meetings

Staff meetings must be consistent and organized. A certain time each day is necessary for a routine. There should be off-season, pre-season, and in-season meetings. Meetings should be meaningful. Respect for family time is a must. People can socialize at another time. Staff meeting need to be business-like and kept to needed times only.

Weekly Meetings

I believe a coaching staff is unified when communication is at its best. Each coach on the staff should have duties. These duties should include equipment, facilities, periods of practice, practice schedule posted on bulletin boards, headsets, outside football equipment, coaching clothes, locker room, laundry, grade checks, and many more. How do we ensure these duties are being performed? You cannot wait until the duty has been neglected and is discovered. I like to have meetings in the morning during days when practices are conducted in the afternoon, or after school if practices are conducted in the morning. Depending on the number of coaches, I would have them equally divided on Monday through Thursday to report what is happening with their duties. It will be amazing how much more gets accomplished when the coaches report on their duties each week. The duty is important regardless if the coach reports on it weekly, but by reporting it does a couple of important things for the staff. First, it lets the staff know what everyone is doing and who oversees each item. Second, the coach understands the duty is valued and they are a viable part of the coaching staff.

Every duty should be important, otherwise do not assign the duty. One of the duties I assigned on my coaching staff was beautification of the field house locker room facility. We had recently built the facility. There was nothing in place outside. I gave the assignment to a top-notch young coach. This fine coach, without any budget, had trees donated to line the road to the facility, planted bushes in front of the facility, had permanent trash receptacles placed at every corner of the building and had welcome mats placed in front of the main doors. What does this have to do with coaching, one might ask. It tells everyone (players, personnel, parents) the facility is important for our players and staff.

I strongly believe the most trusted and competent coaches on a staff will have quality duties outside of field coaching duties. This shows desire to be a team player. This proves value of a person to the team. It shows self-discipline and self-sacrifice. If you want to find the most relied upon coaches, check their duties.

The coach with the beautification duty became one of our most relied on coaches. Today, he serves as the offensive line coach for the NFL Atlanta Falcons. His name is Chris Morgan.

Student Managers

Student managers are valuable. To maintain a well-oiled coaching staff organizational machine, student managers are like gold. The coordinated effort of managers helps keep the flow of practice without mistakes and lack of equipment needs. It is wise to have varsity and sub-varsity managers. All managers need to have a specific role. Inside managers and outside managers help the overall organization flow. Not all teams have this many managers and must combine duties but by having an inside group and outside group, then pre-practice needs are addressed. Players can dress and be assured of proper equipment while on the field managers are setting up drills, placing equipment in proper areas, preparing film, and period exchanges. Just like a coaching staff, a managerial team needs to have a head manager and coordinators, if the program is large.

If your high school or college does not have a staff member handling the custodial duties, then a coach must be assigned. Usually, this coach will supervise the student-managers in this area. Only certified custodians can apply certain disinfectants. Be careful and know the laws.

Equipment Duties

If your school or college does not have an employed person handling equipment, then one your most organized coaches needs this assignment. Equipment is one of the most important areas of a program. There are laws about misappropriation of funds, and rules about amateurism when athletes misuse and take equipment home. Issuing equipment, inventorying equipment, storing equipment, and cleaning equipment are components of coaches handling equipment duties. It is necessary to have checklist for practice and games. Managers can check all these items and handle equipment room needs but an experienced coach should oversee the equipment operation. A well-organized equipment room helps keep a program operating without hitches.

Keep an inventory throughout a season. Every item issued should be labeled and written down on an inventory sheet. A complete inventory sheet should be available throughout a season as well as in an off-season. Purchasing equipment must adhere to school policy on submitting purchase orders and receiving.

When issuing equipment, label every item. Safely store equipment in a legible order. Each size and model should be arranged for easy access. Quality of equipment is more important than quantity. Quality equipment is paramount for satisfaction.

After each season, consideration must be given to which items need reconditioning. Helmets must be logged in when purchased, used, and reconditioned. This is time to give consideration for replacement of depleted supplies, to new equipment or desired supplies for the next season or spring training. If you have kept a running inventory, then this should be a piece of cake. Materials needed for reconditioning should be done immediately after season or after spring training sessions. This ensures equipment will be in stock and ready for season. Check with each position coach and coordinator to make sure needed items are ordered.

Laundry

Keeping equipment clean and safe is a priority for players. Daily laundering of workout clothes is a must. Detergent and proper washing and drying principles must be adhered to. There are proper ways to wash gear. Wet and dirty gear spells disease. Athletes foot, jock rash, and other rashes will prevent players from participation. If playing games on grass fields, game equipment many times will require soaking in a special detergent to remove and prevent staining.

Example Equipment Organization

Director: _____

Budget/Ordering/Inventory Coordinator: _____

- Practice schedule coordination on televisions in locker room (IT-trouble shoot)
- Special team meeting schedule posting
- Special team depth chart posting
- Coaches Clothing Checkout-Ordering
- Dignitaries-Give away

Film Coordinator: _____

    Student Assistant: _____

- Headsets

Equipment Room Supervisor: _____

    Student Assistant: _____

Locker Rooms Supervisor: _____

    Student Assistant: _____

- Offensive practice equipment organization
  Student Assistant: _____

Outside Equipment Supervisor: _____

- Defensive practice equipment organization
- Student Assistant: _____

Clock/Periods: _____

    Student Assistant: _____

Daily Equipment Operations

Equipment/Laundry Room:
1. In-door check in/out
   Responsibilities:

- Equipment Check out-Check in
- Inventory
- Laundry
- Equipment Room Cleanliness
- Equipment numbering
2. Field Equipment
    - Field Set-up and tear down
    - Care and Inventory

Locker Room:

Responsibilities:
- Locker Schematic
- Cleanliness
- Locker Check-Daily

Film-Clock:

Responsibilities:
- Film and Clock operators for practice
- Practice Film
- Help Coach

Student Coaching Assignments

Offense

- Backs-
- Line-
- Receivers-
- Tight Ends-
- Quarterbacks-

Defense

- Corners-
- Safeties-
- Line-
- Linebackers-

Specialists

- Charting-

Training Rules

A player handbook, listing the training rules must be signed before a player can take practice. The rules need to be specific. Rules must be covered in a player-coach meeting and documented. School, state, and national rules must be addressed. If the rule in not enforceable, then we strongly advise to not include the rule in the handbook. If it is a school, state, or national rule, there is not a choice—it must be followed.

To have a successful team, student-athletes need to have self-discipline. Individual participants must learn the importance of self-discipline. Personal sacrifice leads to success. A lack of self-discipline leads to destruction. Conformity to rules and regulations, displaying self-discipline, and having a positive attitude are attributes helping youngsters in the game of life and coaches must be firm and consistent in applying rules and regulations.

The Welch-Bailiff Total Coach Manual: Foundations of Coaching lists what we consider important areas to address in a rules and procedures manual:

- No smoking or vaping.
- No alcoholic beverages for high school or underage students.
- 8 hours of sleep as a minimum, 9 hours preferred.
- No unexcused practice or game absences. Excuse must be prior to practice or game.
- No unexcused practice or game tardiness. Excuse must be prior to practice or game.
- Proper nutrition.
- Show respect to teammates and coaches.
- No theft. Thieves will NOT be tolerated.
- No cutting or altering issued equipment.
- No surprise rule. Do not allow coaches to hear something from someone else about your behavior.
- Do not do anything to embarrass you, your family, your team, or the school.

Enforcement is a problem with handing out a rules and procedures manual. If infractions are handled consistently, then there will be very few problems. If the star athlete gets away with breaking rules, then the rules are worthless. Well-disciplined teams build programs. Today's win might have costs more than you know. Just to keep a player in the program to win a game will end up destroying a program in the future. If you are working at a school valuing wins more than discipline, then you are at the wrong school. A coach must be able to look their players in the face and in a mirror and feel good about themselves. Discipline is the key to having a solid program.

If the rule(s) will not be enforced, then do not list it. For example, we believe nutrition is extremely important but how do you enforce the rule. Emphasizing and asking players about their diet shows coaches care. We recommend keeping it in the rules and procedures manual.

Coaches will sometimes make a rule because they do not think they discover everything the student-athlete does. That is copout. Do not be surprised how other players and parents will inform coaches about rule breakers. Football is a game, but the objective is about building men and understanding winning is a by-product of having a great program.

Also, coaches need to understand they need to devise ways to work with players. The ones breaking rules needed the most help. Many times, football coaches are the players only hope of learning how to become a productive man, husband, father, and community asset. Have ways to work with the youth. Have steps to suspend and have the player to earn their way back on the team. The young man breaking training rules could someday be a leader of a school district, a coach, a teacher, a banker, and on and on. Rest assured, most players not disciplined or cut will more than likely become problems for society. Only as a last resort should a player be dismissed. Do not misunderstand, we do not say to not discipline the young man. Suspension is better than being dismissed. Regardless, coaches have the final word in handling discipline problems.

Physical Examinations and Insurance

Every player by state law must have a physical by a medical professional certified to examine athletes before they practice or play in a game. Most insurance policies are not in place until physical exams have been completed and are on file. It is the head coach's responsibility to ensure all players have a physical exam before they participate.

Insurance coverage is imperative. Student-athletes must provide proof of coverage of insurance. Most states have insurance plans available. In some instances, the participant pays a small premium for the insurance. We recommend school districts purchase umbrella coverage as well.

Conditioning and Early Practices

There is a perception practicing in heat is not good. This is not a true statement. Multiple practices and acclimating to heat (climate conditions) is important for athletes to properly perform. Heat related illnesses are not necessarily derived from intensity and number of practices. The body not being acclimated to weather (climate) conditions is what is harmful. Coaches must be conscious of body core temperature and hydration. Elevated body temperature and dehydration spells danger for athletes. Practicing at various times throughout a day can be helpful in acclimating the body.

The problem with summer and early fall practices is risking the athlete to heat-related illnesses. There is a need to understand how to prevent heat-related illness and have best practice considerations in scheduling practices. Heat and humidity conditions during hot summer and fall practice and games are considerations for athletes. Traditionally, morning and late-afternoon practices are conducted.

Body core temperature is a key component in heat related fatalities. Body acclimation to climate is important for getting in shape. Most coaches conduct morning practice with more conditioning drills requiring a higher level of physical exertion. Evening practice will consist of walk through instructional drills requiring less physical exertion but allowing the body to acclimate to the heat.

Football player deaths have grown significantly in the last decade related to heat illness. Excessively hot and humid conditions, equipment restricting cooling of the body, and intense workouts are factors contributing to heat-related illnesses. Consequently, early season practice times are a critical component in considering practice schedules. Football practices begin in late summer, which is traditionally the hottest time of the year. Intensity of workouts during these extreme conditions causes the body temperature to rise (Mazerolle, Casa, & Casa, 2009). Armstrong et al. (2010) indicated athletes run a risk of body overheating during dog days of summer. The intensity of workouts and multiple practice sessions on consecutive days causes extreme body stress (Mazerolle et al., 2009). This reminds me of a car engine. When temperatures are cool, engines are not stressed. If put under stress during extreme temperatures, engines many times will overheat.

Why have multiple practices? Given the intense physical sport nature and technical demands of integrating specific positions into a team concept, it is common for preseason practices to provide repetitious practices and conditioning intensity. Multiple practice sessions physically prepare athletes for a grueling season by acclimating their body to weather conditions they will participate in. It is recommended to conduct these practices during cooler times.

Exertional heatstroke (EHS) results in sudden death among athletes (Armstrong et al., 2010). Gradually adding equipment to athletes allows bodies to acclimate to heat, which is a preventive measure against heat stroke. The first 4 days of practice in Texas is an acclimation period and only allows a helmet to be worn as protective equipment (UIL, 2020b). This allows athletes to gradually acclimate their bodies to climate conditions. Lack of acclimatization, poor aerobic fitness, excess body fat, and extreme motivation to push a body to exhaustive limits have increased rates of heat related illnesses (Mazerolle et al., 2009). Virtually all exertional heatstroke deaths occur among non-acclimatized players during initial summer practices. Deaths due to exertional heatstroke are preventable with prompt diagnoses and treatment (Armstrong et al., 2010). Cold-water immersion must be immediate, and body temperature reduced to prevent death. Athletic trainers and or coaches must organize a prevention program of ice whirlpools, iced towels, and cool water during practice sessions.

The addition of shoulder pads, hip pads, and kneepads increase core body temperatures. The amount of body surface covered is an important consideration, especially during hot practice sessions. Body surface, which is covered, impairs dissipation. In Texas, protective equipment (shoulder pads, hip pads, and kneepads) cannot be worn until after an athlete has participated in a 4-day acclimation period (UIL, 2020b).

It is preferable to have a licensed trainer at practices and it is a must to have measures in place to serve athletes should a problem arise.

Early Fall Training–Conditioning

The body conditioning program is muscular strength conditioning and cardiovascular endurance. The muscular strength conditioning program serves as a pre-conditioner for athletes. The principle is to overload the body. Using weights to condition athletes speeds up the conditioning process. Throughout the entire year, a weight program prepares athletes for their seasons. In-season and off-season weight program are necessary to maximize an athlete's ability to perform. All body parts should be exercised emphasizing muscles particularly used for specific sports. Example: A baseball pitcher lifts weights for arms and shoulders different than an offensive and defensive lineman. Offensive linemen build their upper bodies much different than a long-distance track and field athlete. Trained strength coaches will understand all these needs. Some schools rely on a coach. Consequently, having thorough knowledge of weight training is necessary for all coaches.

Cardiovascular endurance is also a year-round program. Prior to a season, athletes should employ short sprints. These are preferred to long distance training, although long distance training is preferred during months prior to season. Practices should include fast movements, quick sprints such as kickoff and punt returns. Running or defending routes all help condition football players. Charging sleds, pass blocking, and rushing help prepare linemen. The practices should be conducted in a way so that sprints after practice are not necessary.

The extent and type of seasonal conditioning efforts are to maintain what has already been instilled in a player. If a player comes into a season physically ill-prepared, doom is inevitable.

Conditioning During a Season

Maintain, maintain, maintain, some coaches lose in this area. Weight conditioning and cardiovascular endurance must be maintained for athletes to maximize abilities throughout a season. Time and time again, I hear how a team could have been good, but they lost some good players to injuries. Physically fit and conditioned teams have better season results (B. Powel, personal communication, January 4, 2018). How many days should a team lift weights during a season? That all depends on type of lifts and time given to weight conditioning. At least 2 days per week is recommended but some coaches lift 5 days a week emphasizing different body parts each day.

Running, again, short burst and position specific conditioning is recommended. Participate like you play in a game. Running a certain amount of consecutive plays to simulate a game is good conditioning work.

Game and Practice Film

The changes in technology are remarkable. Practice and game plans can be viewed online. Team plays are visual. With HUDL and other programs, live footage is available as soon as a play has been conducted. How do coaches show film to teams? Showing film is an asset in teaching and correcting players. Players now have access to immediately view practice or game film.

I believe there are two general uses for film: (a) review by coaches for instruction and correction and (b) review by team members.

Team Meetings

This is a must. The culture of a team is prevalent in team meetings. The head coach sets the tone. Assistant coaches and players should be attentive. Put the cell phones up. It is best to not allow players to have a cell phone at a team meeting unless it is an emergency. The number and length of meeting will vary. Quality and experienced teams do not need to meet as much as young, inexperienced teams. Short sessions tend to work best.

To have a good team meeting, you need to remember, normal humans have a hard time maintaining attention for over 3 minutes. Adapt the meetings accordingly. Have something to break the monotony. Raise your voice. Have interaction. Turn on the lights and check everyone if lights are off while watching film.

Basic team meetings: (game week)

- Monday–prior to practice. Brief scouting report of opponent, then walk through with offense and defense. Address concerns and things to work on as a team.
- Thursday–review how we will defeat our opponent. Address travel and expectations of arrival. Any concerns of a home or away contest (equipment, locker rooms, action of their players, fans, etc.)
- Saturday–after Friday night game. Cover what the team did well in all three phases. Announce players of the week. Briefly talk about preparing for next opponent.

Conflict Management

The head coach ensures all coaches provide *constructive criticism* to players. Head coaches must do the same to assistant coaches to build team comradery. Provide advice about how to give criticism in a way that will enable the criticism to be heard and acted upon. Other areas of criticism for the head coach to address:

- Dealing with criticism–Explain how to hear and accept criticism.
- Giving and receiving feedback.
- How to complain (Effectively)–provide some useful techniques on how to make a complaint that will be heard and acted upon.
- Mediation skills.
- Sometimes informal conflict resolution is not enough.
- Know when it is time to step away from a conflict situation and ask someone more skilled to mediate?

Trust the assistant coaches. There was a player with tremendous potential but for whatever reason I was not connecting with him. I was to the point of letting the player go. Our defensive coordinator, Howard McMahan, asked for permission to handle the player and requested I stay away. I had a lot of faith and trust in Howard, so I agreed. The player responded well. He became a captain on our team, received all-state honors, and eventually received a Division I scholarship. The player was really a great kid. We liked each other well when we learned how to work together. TRUST other coaches to be part of solutions.

CHAPTER SIX:
Leading the Way

A head coach "is a professional at training and developing athletes" ("Head coach," 2020, para. 1). They hold a "public profile and are paid more than other coaches" for these additional responsibilities (para. 1). The head coach position is a miniature schematic of the athletic director position. Many head coaches serve as the athletic director.

Game Planning

Coaches' offices usually have big dry erase boards. Larger school districts will have offensive and defensive meeting rooms. The board or boards will have rows and rows of numbers and words handwritten in a language of football.

Typical categories will be codes like 3rd and 1-2; 3rd and 3-6; Red Zone; Goal Line.

Putting together a game plan is a complexed exercise. Coaches analyze an opponent's tendencies and patterns to create a game plan. From reviewing film, rosters, injuries, and team strengths and weaknesses, coaches determining how best to exploit an opponent. The process considers what opponents do. What is their bread and butter and when and where do they run certain plays? Then coaches will figure out the best plays to run offensively and defense alignments (with stunts and blitzes) for the upcoming game. All special teams will do likewise.

The operation of putting together a game plan varies from staff to staff and coach to coach, but the process is usually the same.

Game Plan Preparation

Summer game-planning prepares for the first game. Staffs will also prepare for a team they consider a must win. Many staffs plan for the first three opponents as well.

During the season, game planning begins a week before leading up to a game. One way high school coaches weekly game plan is to have sub-varsity assistants breakdown film on the next opponent.

Today, recording plays is on digital recordings, and computer software from companies such as XOS and on-screen labeling. Plays are sorted by down and distance and labeled. Defenses would include the number of defensive backs, linebackers, and linemen on the field. The front—specific players lined up over offensive linemen and stunts, coverage—specific players in secondary and identify coverages, and pressure—which players are blitzing and from where.

Sunday (after church), about 2:00 pm, prepare the game plan. Go home and rest at 5:00 pm.

Monday

The results of Saturday and Sunday's game-planning are implemented on the practice field. Make corrections from last week's game and game plan for this week's opponent. Coaches, after practice, put final touches on the game plan.

Tuesday–Wednesday

Full contact practice. Review game plan plays in all three areas. Usually all three groups—offense, defense, and special teams—will practice half of the game plan on Tuesday and the other half of the game plan on Wednesday. Of course, opponents are preparing for our teams' strengths and weaknesses as well. Develop an opponent surprise sheet. List plays and defenses detected potentially to hurt the team. Implement at different times in practice to prepare all three groups.

After practice, coaches review the practice film. Prepare for the next day's practice. Time to add to or subtract from the game plans. Be sure to document how many repetitions each play was performed in practice. Coaches cannot expect players to perform plays they did not practice.

Thursday

Walk-through all three groups and practice extras—on-side kicks, hands team, hail Mary, hurry-up offense, slow-down defense, and many others. Have a check list.

Friday

Game day. Work the plan to perfection. Win.

Saturday

Players: Watch Friday night's game film, lift weights, jog to get the blood flowing, then go home and rest.

Coaches: Watch half of Friday night's film together as a staff (Assistants should watch all game film and grade their players). Start watching opponents' film and reviewing scouts and sub-varsity coaches' breakdown of film. At 4:00 pm, go home and rest, spend time with family.

Film Breakdown

This is a basic way to break down the previous week's game film. This is an example for football. Each sport is similar in design.

The Offense

Identify and grade each position player. Did they complete their assignment on each play? In addition, here are 14 items to look for when evaluating offensive units and players:

1. Speed off the ball.
2. Intensity of play performance.
3. Position technique on each play for all positions.
4. Hustle. How many players are in the last frame of film when play is over?
5. Which line of scrimmage are we playing on, offensive or defensive side?
6. Blitz pickup?
7. Stunt pickup?
8. Ball handling?
9. Were there any fumbles?
10. How many yards after contact?
11. Quarterback protection.
12. Timing of routes?
13. Busted plays?
14. Any loafs?

The Defense

Like offense. Do players complete their assignments every play? In addition, here are 17 items to look for when evaluating offensive units and players:

1. Speed and intensity after snap.
2. Position technique?
3. The ability to get off blocks and swarm to the football. How many in last frame of play on film?
4. LOS. Who won the line of scrimmage?
5. Pre snap alignment.
6. Ability to tackle in space.
7. Ability to tackle out of space.
8. The speed play recognition.
9. Fooled on any trick plays.
10. Solo tackles.
11. Team tackles.
12. Pass coverage.
13. How many Quarterback pressures?
14. Are the pursuit angles correct?
15. Control ball tempo? Did we perform slow down defense perfectly?
16. How many times did they jump offsides?
17. How many busted assignments? Count every bust. There could be three on one play.

Special Teams

Evaluating coverage teams.

1. Punt snap. Time of snap to kick.
2. Punter operation to get punt off.
3. Ability to protect the punter.
4. Distance and height of each punt.
5. Punt coverage. How fast and disciplined is the coverage.
6. Tackling ability.

Evaluating the kickoff coverage team.

1. How fast and disciplined coverage.
2. Ability to tackle and the skill level of kicker.
3. Hang time.

Evaluating return team.

1. Operation and discipline of return.
2. Stay on blocks.
3. Speed of returner.
4. Average on each return.

Evaluating field goal and PAT team.

1. Speed of snap to kick.
2. Blocking techniques.
3. Field goal range.
4. Height of ball off tee.
5. Operation of kick.
6. Does FG block team have designated block angles?
7. Does FG block team have safeties on each side of ball?

Strategies

All sports have strategies and tactics. This is called a game plan, which was covered previously. Strategies include plays and tactics that are developed to accentuate players and abilities of your team. Coaches adjusting schemes to available talent is much better than players—without the ability to perform certain techniques—trying to perform what a coach likes to do. Example: A small basketball team would perform a run and gun style of play versus a taller, slower team using a deliberate setup game.

A run and shoot offense needs a special quarterback. A running quarterback is better suited in a run-style offense.

Proficiency of Technology of Sport

Analysis/Quality Control

This intensive program details a unique and powerful approach to integrating a business and technology strategy and to developing profitable ventures and technologies. Participants are introduced to a set of tools to identify high-leverage projects, match product strategy to market dynamics, capture market value, and change organizational capabilities to reflect evolving markets and technological dynamics.

Hiring Practices

- How to hire the right employee.
- Termination Practices: How to document legal implications. The "Termination without Tears" process advocates a win-win for both parties involved (Thompson, 2014). Never surprise an employee at the end of the year. Notify the employee of deficiencies. Work, work, work to assist the employee to correct the deficiencies (growth plan). If necessary, find another job suitable for employee to be successful.

Leadership of the Head Coach

- Leadership **PRIDE**: **P**assion, **R**espect, **I**nnovation, **D**etermination, **E**xcellence.
- Principals of Value-Based Leadership: Servanthood, Thankfulness, Accountability, Humility, Passion
- Unity: The team concept (**T**ogether **E**veryone **A**chieves **M**ore).

Recommended Books on Leadership: Good to Great and Developing the Moral Component of Authentic Leadership

Good to Great by Jim Collins (2001)

> Why do some companies make the leap to great and others don't? This book is known as a modern classic on management theory. Jim Collins identifies and evaluates the factors and variables that allow a small fraction of companies (companies looked at for 15 year accumulative stock returns and the returns had to have three times the market share to qualify as great) to make the transition from good to great ("Good to great," 2016; Garner, 2015). Collins used 15 years so a company could not be a one hit wonder. To put this in perspective, General Electric was thought to be the best company in America, but it only outperformed the market by 2.8 times over 15 years from 1985-2000. "Great" is operationally defined according to several metrics, including financial performance that exceeded the market average by several orders of magnitude over a sustained period. Using these criteria, Collins and his research team catalogued the business literature identifying a handful of companies that fulfilled their predetermined criteria for greatness. Then, the identifying characteristics that differentiated these "great" companies from their competitors were quantified and analyzed. One theme that links together all of Collins' arguments is the need to define a narrowly focused objective and field of competency and then

focus all of the company's established resources toward that area of strength. Collin warns that straying too far from a company's strengths will keep the company from attaining greatness.

Collins states that the problem for good companies not becoming great is focusing on what the company is best at and concentrating on that area ("Good to great," 2016; Garner, 2015). Being too diverse can keep a company from being great in the area the company is best at. The company leaders must know what they can be the best at and make decisions to be the best in the world.

The purpose of the book is to help leaders understand what the companies' hedgehog concept is. A great company must know their "hedgehog" concept and how to lead as a humble Level 5 leader.

Good is the enemy of great. Collins lays out the criteria his research team used in selecting the companies ("Good to great," 2016; Garner, 2015). The most important factor in the selection process was a period of growth and sustained success that far outpaced the market or industry average. Based on the stated criteria, the companies that were selected for the inclusion were Abbott, Fannie Mae, Circuit City, Gillette, Kimberly-Clark, Kroger, Nucor, Phillip Morris, Pitney Bowes, Walgreens, and Wells Fargo. Collins offers a few of the most significant findings gleaned in the study. There are many indications that the factors such as the CEO compensation, technology, mergers and acquisitions, and change management initiatives played relatively minor roles in fostering the Good to Great process. Instead, Collins found that successes in the three main areas: disciplined people, discipline thought, and disciplined action. These were the most significant factors in determining a company's ability to achieve greatness.

Level 5 leadership. Collins identifies and explains the factors and variables that differentiate good to great companies ("Good to great," 2016; Garner, 2015). One of the most significant differences is the quality and nature of leadership in the firm. Collins did not want the research team to consider leadership, but they could not get away from leadership, leadership continued to come to the forefront. Collins identified this level of leadership "Level 5" leadership. Level 5 hierarchy ranges from merely competent supervision to strategic executive decision-making. By studying the behaviors and attitudes of the Level 5 leaders, Collins found that many of those classified in this group displayed an unusual mix of intense determination and profound humility. These leaders often have a long-term personal sense of investment in the company and its successes, often through a career-spanning climb up the company's ranks. The personal ego and individual financial gain are not as important as the long-term benefit of the TEAM and the company to true Level 5 leaders. Bringing in a "celebrity" CEO like Lee Iacocca to turn around a failing firm is usually not conducive to fostering the transition from Good to Great. What happened to Chrysler after he left (crashed)?

First who, then what. The concept of the leadership team ("Good to great," 2016; Garner, 2015). Secure high quality, high-talent individuals with Level 5 leadership abilities, before a strategy can be developed. With the right people in the right positions, Collins contends that many management problems, that plague companies and sap valuable resources, will automatically go away. Firms that make the Good to Great transition find it worthwhile to expend extra energy and time on personnel searches and decision-making. Maintaining rigorousness in all personnel decisions. Move potential failing employees and managers to new positions and remove personnel that are not actively contributing (Get the right people on the bus and the wrong ones off the bus before deciding where the bus is to go). This will save time in the end.

Confront the brutal facts, yet never lose faith. Companies that make the transition from Good to Great have the willingness to identify and access defining facts in the company and in the larger business environment ("Good to great," 2016; Garner, 2015). In today's market, trends in consumer preferences are constantly changing, and the inability to keep pace with these changes often results in company failure. Using the example of an extended comparative analysis of Kroger and A & P, Collins observes that Kroger recognized the trend towards modernization in the grocery industry and adjusted its business model accordingly, although doing so required a complete transformation of the company and its stores. A & P resisted large-scale changes and guaranteed its own demise. Collins outlined a four-step process to promote emerging trends and potential problems: 1) Lead with questions, not answers; 2) Engage in dialogue and debate, not coercion; 3) Conduct autopsies without blame; and 4) Build red flag mechanisms that turn information into information that cannot be ignored.

The hedgehog concept has three circles. Collins uses the metaphor of the hedgehog to illustrate the principle that simple can sometimes lead to greatness ("Good to great," 2016; Garner, 2015). When confronted by predators, the hedgehog response is to roll up into a ball. While other predators, such as a fox, may be impressively clever, few can devise a strategy that is effective enough to overcome the hedgehog's simple, repetitive response. Three circles identify what the company is best at: a) Determine what you can do best and be the best in the world at; b) Determine what drives your economic engine; and c) Determine what you are deeply passionate about.

A culture of discipline must be developed, but not an authoritarian environment. An organization in which each manager and-staff member is driven by an unrelenting inner sense of determination ("Good to great," 2016; Garner, 2015). In this type of organization, each member functions as an entrepreneur, with a personal investment in both work and company success. This discipline will manifest in a high standard of quality of work produced by managers and employees alike, but its most significant outcome is fanatical devotion to objectives. Disciplined workers will be better equipped to adhere to these goals with a single-minded intensity that will foster the transformation from Good to Great. Each member is afforded a personal empowerment and latitude that is necessary to ensure that they will be able to go extremes to bring a company envisioned objectives into existence.

Technology accelerators need to be explored. Collins cautions that technology should not be regarded as a potential panacea for all that ails a company ("Good to great," 2016; Garner, 2015). Good to Great companies approach the prospect of new and emerging technologies with the same prudence and careful deliberation that characterizes all their other business in a manner that is reflective to their hedgehog concepts decisions.

Pause, think, crawl, walk, and run is what Collins says must happen in an organization ("Good to great," 2016; Garner, 2015). Then he explains the flywheel and the doom loop. Two cycles that demonstrate the way decisions tend to accumulate in either advantageous or disadvantageous manner. Both accrue over time. Despite the popular misconception that business success or failure often occurs suddenly, Collins asserts that it more typically occurs over a course of years, and that both transpire after sufficient positive or negative momentum has been accrued. The flywheel effect is the cycle turning and turning and building power as it turns. Results are the accumulation of tangible positive outcomes, which serves as energy to staff and team. In contrast, the doom loop is characterized by reactive decision-making, an overextension into too many diverse areas of concentration, following short-lived trends, frequent changes in leadership and personnel, loss of morale, and disappointing results.

How do we move from good to great? Collins makes a connection between this book and his previous work, Built to Last ("Good to great," 2016; Garner, 2015). He contends that companies need a set of core values to achieve the kind of long-term, sustainable success that may lead to greatness. Companies need to exist for a higher purpose than mere profit generation to transcend the category of merely good. To be the BEST at what they do and consistently achieve success, team members must be equally dedicated.

Collins leadership principles relate to Jesus. Jesus was a humble leader. He focused on a vision to help save the lost and spread the message of life. This book is an example of Level 5 leaders, leaders that focus on others, the vision, the mission, and not themselves ("Good to great," 2016; Garner, 2015). Money does not drive the engine, self-gain does not drive the engine, but accomplishment for the company drives the engine. Making hard decisions, taking careful time to make decisions, never forgetting the goal. Jesus knew the mission and was willing to give His life for the WIN. Have faith the right will prevail. "Do right and right will prevail."

How would a leader use this book (examples)? A leader must be willing to reorganize the organization after thorough evaluation of skills and talents. Willing to fire "dead" weight that is hurting the company, people who are not contributing. Be slow to react. Use the "team's" input and debate to make decisions. Understand what the company is best at, what economically fuels the engine, and what "we" are passionate about. Get the right people on the bus, in the right seats, and the wrong people off the bus. Collins says leaders need to change-move from dictator (boss) to leader ("Good to great," 2016; Garner, 2015). Supply workers and employees, empower them, trust them, and get out of the way; however, supervise, guide, and instruct.

- Do not let technology drive the engine–Pause, think, crawl, walk, run. Be willing to make major changes that are in-line with the hedgehog concept.

- Decision-making-team work–Collaboration, delegation, and trust.

- Ethics–Be honest in transitions and transactions with employees. Be non-judgmental—we all make mistakes and mistakes are evidence that someone tried.

- Law–Know what the company can and cannot do. Do not break the law for short-term gain.

- Leadership–Level 5 leaders are humble, often come up through the ranks and are passionate about company success not individual success.

- Perspective–Know what drives the company, get the right employees on the bus (talented/skilled), and get the wrong ones off (they will suck the life out of the company). Be willing to make needed changes but only after thorough collaborative thought.

- Relationships–This kind of humble leadership brings forth a team of people who unite as FAMILY. Family WINS. Accept differences and other talents, realizing it takes all kinds to succeed.

- Research–Facts not opinions. Success tells the story if it is sustained—long-term success. Look at other companies, compare results, and continually learn.

- Resources–Humble leaders get the right people hired, collaborate planning (confront the brutal facts), determine the hedgehog, understand the role of discipline, realize technology can help, have momentum, and appreciate success.

- Systems–In education, document to get rid of dead weight, data-data-data, hire quality people, put a TEAM together to be the administrative team, and know your community.

"Developing the Moral Component of Authentic Leadership" by May et al. (2003).

According to May et al. (2003), leaders are more aware of moral issues if they possess a level of moral capacity that is heightened. Leaders should be ethically responsible to those who are a part of the organization, handle ethical issues, and learn from the past. There are some leaders who decide to act unethically for very legitimate reasons. Ethical leaders need the courage to overcome the temptation to act unethically, regardless of the pressures they receive. To overcome the temptation, leaders must be resilient in the way they handle moral issues. The leaders who can abstain from being unethical will become the moral leader they originally sought to be.

The authors describe authentic leadership as the leader knowing himself and being transparent in the way they lead every day (May et al., 2003). Authentic leadership is defined "as a positive construct, descriptive words include genuine, reliable, trustworthy, real, and veritable" (Luthans & Avolio, as cited in May et al., 2003, p. 2). The bottom line is for a person to become an authentic leader, they must know and be true to themselves. Authentic leaders possess a high moral capacity.

At the center of the authentic leader is an authentic person (May et al., 2003). The authentic person must be well aware of what they believe in and what they stand for. An authentic person is completely immersed in their core beliefs and values. An authentic leader conveys their core values and beliefs in every situation they face. They do this because they have a fundamental sense of who they are. Authentic leaders mean what they say and say what they mean.

Authentic leaders ultimately shape their organization (May et al., 2003). They shape it by creating an environment in which employees feel safe and cared for. Employees feel their worth and know they are supported. Oftentimes when people are open and honest about a situation, they are called whistleblowers. In an authentically led organization, these people are praised and seen as the heroes in hopes that others will emulate this same behavior. When an organization is led in this manner, its success will be automatic. Its reputation will bring more authentic leaders to work.

Authentic leaders must make decision while being aware that the decision could bring harm to them or their organization (May et al., 2003). The authors give six characteristics in relation to the intensity of a moral issue—consequences vary for those involved, consequences may or may not occur, when consequences occur depends, individuals involved vary in relation to the leader, consequences may effect a few people or many, and consensus may differ in regards to what others think the leader should do. These factors influence the decision-making process in dealing with a given moral issue.

A case study was presented and evaluated for the different ethical and moral issues contained therein (May et al., 2003). A company evaluated its financial statements and found that a large amount of the billing and shipments were recorded incorrectly. The manager was faced with a difficult situation as to how to rectify the company's financial statements. In appraising the case study, the authors describe three steps in the decision-making process. First an authentic leader recognizes the presence of a moral dilemma. Second, the leader transparently evaluates all of the alternatives in solving the problem. And lastly, the leader develops intentions to act appropriately in dealing with the situation.

The first step in the decision-making process is recognizing that a moral issue is present (May et al., 2003). It is up to the leader to determine if a moral dilemma is in the situation. In this step, the authentic leader will draw upon past experiences and core value and beliefs to determine the exact issue. The leader's moral capacity also influences the decision made in a situation. Moral capacity is defined as how the leader builds his/her role in the organization. It also involves their perspective-taking ability, and prior experience in dealing with moral issues. Authentic leaders have a highly developed sense of responsibility to do what is right. They realize that their behavior and decision greatly impact their organization. Authentic leaders are able to view a situation from different perspectives. This helps them be able to fully evaluate all the areas in which a moral dilemma is present.

Once the authentic leader determines that the situation does present a moral dilemma, he or she must then evaluate all the possible alternatives for dealing with the situation (May et al., 2003). Instead of focusing on the outcome, an authentic leader focuses on reasoning through possible outcomes and also tries to be as open and honest as they can be in these deliberations. The authentic leader is also concerned with how the outcomes can affect all the stakeholders. They settle on an outcome that is not self-serving, rather an outcome that is fair and just and because it boasts the best course of action for the organization.

After the leader has determined the appropriate solution to the problem, he or she acts in accordance with how they evaluated the problem to begin with (May et al., 2003). By this, the authentic leader will "do the right thing" for the organization and act authentically (p. 9). The case study concludes with the manager deciding to be open about the financial errors that were made to correct the situation. He informed all the stakeholders and evaluated possible solutions for correcting the financial statements. The leader realized that this situation could have negative consequences for himself, but he felt that confronting the issue was in the best interest of the company. The manager first spoke to his company's leadership team and presented the problem to them. While the stakeholders in the company were disappointed that the financial problems had occurred, they applauded his honesty in handling the problem. The manager took several steps in correcting the problems. He apologized to the company's customers for problems and inconsistencies they may have encountered due to the company's error. He also amended financial statements that had been sent to the IRS so that any discrepancies in the company's finances would be corrected. In this challenging process, the manager of the company showed resilient, ethical behavior in how he led the company through a trying time.

True authentic behavior is composed of moral action, moral courage, sustainable authentic behavior, and moral resiliency (May et al., 2003). In an authentically led organization, ethical behavior is praised, not discouraged. Moral courage is the leader's will to withstand pressures and act in accordance with core values and beliefs. If a leader is confident then usually their moral courage is higher. A leader must also strive to continue to act authentically. This type of behavior should not be a one-time deal. A leader should commit to behaving ethically always. Moral resiliency is the ability to act ethically in the face of adversity or trials. Leaders will discover more self-worth when they are able to work through difficulty.

Authentic leadership skills can also be developed (May et al., 2003). To build moral capacity leaders should self-reflect about the roles they have in their organization. Leaders can also be trained to reason through the alternative solutions to make the best possible choice. Moral courage can be developed through role playing in a moral dilemma and analyzing the various outcomes. Moral resiliency can be established by mentoring. Another leader of moral character can mentor a new leader. Resiliency is also developed by going through real moral dilemmas and coming out the other side of the situation having made an ethical choice. Several other factors play into authentic leadership development. Organizations must select leaders who are motivated to be authentic. Support must also be given to these leaders in making ethical decisions, and leaders should be rewarded when they do make authentic, moral decisions. The authors' hope in writing this article was to encourage ethical and moral behavior in organizations and also to show the ways in which moral behavior can be developed in the workplace.

FSCC-KWU

COURSE
FOUR

CHAPTER SEVEN:
The Athletic Director

The athletic director is the leader of the athletic department (Angst, 2019). They oversee budgeting, marketing, accomplishing specific growth goals, employee evaluations, and implementing organizational and infrastructural improvements. Most importantly, athletic directors are the liaison between athletics and academics. They work in association with superintendents and college presidents to align goals and ideals. Athletic directors also act as an embodiment of the school's overarching beliefs.

Athletic directors have multiple unique responsibilities, which they must balance carefully. For example, in a single day, an athletic director may attend financial meetings, arrange field reservations, purchase specific athletic resources, and implement specific improvements or policy changes.

One of the most important skills an athletic director can possess is effective decision-making. This can be especially crucial when defining the goals and the future of the department. Athletic directors are the face of their departments, demonstrating the ability to steer their programs in a direction they see fit.

Athletic directors have several substantial duties and responsibilities, including helping students to maintain an educational and athletic balance, setting the creative vision for their department, and working with top administrators to manage their department's resources and ongoing organizational efforts. These organizational responsibilities include hiring coaching staff, promoting the athletic programs, maintaining facilities, and coordinating with administrative staff. Athletic departments can have a substantial impact on the revenue and enrollment of a learning institution, so its image needs to positively reflect the school or university.

Role and Responsibilities

Common high school athletic director description.

JOB TITLE: Athletic Director-High School	WAGE/HOUR STATUS: Exempt
REPORTS TO: Superintendent (large school)	PAY GRADE: Negotiable
DEPT./SCHOOL: Athletics	DATE REVISED: 1-28-02 CCISD

PRIMARY PURPOSE:

Direct and manage the overall program of extracurricular athletics for the district. Provide each student an opportunity to participate in an extracurricular athletic activity and ensure compliance with all state, UIL, and local requirements.

QUALIFICATIONS:

>Education/Certification:
>Bachelor's degree
>Valid Texas teaching certificate
>
>Special Knowledge/Skills:
>Knowledge of the overall operations of an athletic program
>Ability to manage budget and personnel
>Strong communication, public relations, and interpersonal skills
>Knowledge of state and UIL policies governing athletics
>
>Experience:
>Five years teaching and coaching experience

MAJOR RESPONSIBILITIES AND DUTIES:

1. Direct and manage the district's athletic program and facilities.

2. Implement the policies established by federal and state laws, State Board of Education rule, UIL rules, and the local board policy in athletics.

3. Ensure that programs are cost effective and that funds are managed prudently.

4. Compile budgets and cost estimates based on documented program needs.

5. Recruit, train, and supervise all athletic department personnel and make sound recommendations relative to personnel placement, assignment, retention, discipline, and dismissal.

6. Evaluate job performance of employees to ensure effectiveness.

7. Prepare, review, and revise job descriptions in athletic department.

8. Prepare and approve all interscholastic game schedules.

9. Arrange transportation, lodging, and meals for out-of-town athletic events.

10. Manage district game operations by directing ticket sales, employing game officials, and ensuring preparation of facilities.

11. Establish the physical and academic requirements of eligibility for participation in each sport and verify each athlete's eligibility.

12. Enforce the district's student management policies and expected student behavior related to athletic program.

13. Maintain an active program that promotes good sportsmanship and student development.

14. Establish and maintain open lines of communication by conducting conferences with parents, students, principals, and teachers.

15. Oversee process of cleaning, repairing, and storage of all athletic equipment.

16. Coordinate the use of all athletic facilities by groups outside of the school.

17. Plan, organize, and supervise all athletic awards programs.

18. Obtain and use evaluative findings, including student achievement data, to examine athletic program effectiveness and ensure that program renewal is continuous and responsive to student needs.

19. Recommend policies directed toward program improvement.

20. Compile, maintain, and file all reports, records, and other documents required.

SUPERVISORY RESPONSIBILITIES:

Supervise and evaluate the performance of coaches, and secretary assigned to the athletics department.

WORKING CONDITIONS:

Mental Demands:

> Ability to communicate effectively (verbal and written); interpret policy, procedures, and data; coordinate district functions; and maintain emotional control under stress.

Physical Demands/Environmental Factors:

> Frequent district and statewide travel; frequent prolonged and irregular hours.

Improve Internal and External Communication

Internal communication is a two-way street. Communication must flow both ways. Giving feedback to your employees is important and necessary to operate a consistent athletic department. Having honest and open communication builds trust. This trustworthy culture encourages dialogue between teams and individuals. When staff members understand their role and expectations, they will work for success.

Demonstrate knowledge in submitting required reports to the athletic department on time: before, during, and after the season.

Goals and Objectives

The (School District) recognizes and promotes the priority of academics within the athletic programs. While athletics are an important part of education, academic success remains the primary objective. The athletic program is designed to enhance academic achievement and should never interfere with opportunities for academic success. To compliment the personal and academic growth of our students, the primary objectives of our athletic programs and coaches shall be to

- Teach positive attitudes, proper habits, knowledge, and skills.
- Develop student abilities through healthy competition.
- Bring about the realizations in the students that competition is a privilege that carries definite responsibilities.
- Develop an interest in sports that will carry over into adult life.
- Represent the school/district in a manner that brings respect for the school and each individual participant.
- Develop a healthy attitude towards opponents, realizing that they deserve our most sincere effort to emerge victorious while simultaneously understanding that their purpose is to defeat us in a healthy, sporting encounter.
- Allow every individual the maximum opportunity to participate in an activity while recognizing that sports, like life, is a competitive situation in which some will excel, some will succeed, some will fail, and all will benefit merely by being participants.
- Emphasize priority of academics and maintain and communicate a philosophy that athletics is a part of the education and character development of our students.

Professional Standards of Conduct

- Sportsmanship is the standard of our athletic department.
- Our district promotes good sportsmanship among athletes, parents, fans, and coaches. To help ensure that we represent our school and community with dignity, the coach is expected to:
  - Exemplify behavior that is representative of the educational staff of the school and a credit to the teaching profession.
  - Demonstrate high ideals, good habits, and desirable attitudes in personal behavior and demand the same standard of the players.
  - Recognize that the purpose of competition is to promote the physical, mental, social, and emotional well-being of the individual players and that the most important values of competition are derived from playing the game fairly.
  - Be a modest winner and gracious loser.
  - Always maintain self-control, accepting adverse decisions without undue public display of emotion or dissatisfaction.

- o Pay close attention to the physical condition and well-being of the players, refusing to jeopardize the health of an individual for the sake of improving his/her team's chances to win.
- o Teach athletes that it is better to lose fairly than to win unfairly.
- o Prohibit gambling, profanity, abusive language, and similar violations.
- o Refuse to disparage an opponent, an official, or others associated with sports activities and discourage gossip and questionable rumors concerning them.

Code of Ethics

- To ensure that our coaches serve as positive role models in the education of the student athletes. The (ISD) recognizes the code of ethics established by the (District) Principal's Association. In addition, the (District) has adopted its own code of ethics for coaches. As a coach with the (District), you shall:
  - o Constantly uphold the honor and dignity of the teaching profession. In all personal contact with the student athlete, officials, athletic directors, school administrators, the state high school athletic association, the media, and the public. The coach shall strive to set an example of the highest ethical and moral character, behavior, and leadership.
  - o Support the school's position on academic importance and make every effort to accommodate students' needs as they balance academics with athletic activities.
  - o Demonstrate and encourage respect for the individual personality and integrity of each student athlete.
  - o Never place the value of winning or disappointment of defeat above the value of character building. Model and encourage the highest standard of conduct in both victory and defeat.
  - o Support and enforce school and training rules for the prevention of drug, alcohol and tobacco use and abuse, and under no circumstances authorize the use of these substances.
  - o Promote the entire interscholastic program of the school and direct his or her program in harmony with the total school program. Encourage the highest standards of academic achievement among team members.
  - o Be thoroughly acquainted with contest, state, league, and local rules, and always abide by the letter and spirit of these rules.
  - o Actively use his/her influence to enhance sportsmanship by participants and spectators.
  - o Respect and support contest officials, and refrain from publicly criticizing officials or indulging in conduct which will incite players or spectators against the officials or against each other.
  - o Model and promote ethical relations among coaches, student athletes, spectators, and members of the rival team. Meet and exchange friendly greetings with the rival coach(es) to set the correct tone for the event, before and after contests. Refrain from publicly criticizing coaches, players, or spectators.
  - o Refrain from exerting pressure on faculty members to give student athletes special consideration.

- Refrain from scouting opponents by any other means than those adopted by the state high school athletic association and the league.
- Encourage the highest standard of conduct among student athletes and strive to create an environment where hazing is deemed unacceptable behavior by all team members. Never condone hazing behavior.
- Behave and dress professionally both on and off the field/court in the presence of students. Inappropriate attire, use of profanity, and vulgar/offensive language are prohibited.
- Demonstrate a mastery of and continuing interest in coaching through professional improvement.
- Establish sound training rules that seek to encourage and support good health habits among team members.
- Be attentive to the first aid needs of student athletes and strive to provide an environment free of safety hazards.

Relationships with Student-Athletes

- It is critical that coaches know where to draw the line with student athletes between coach and friend. It is equally important that coaches recognize behaviors, actions, gestures, or comments towards student athletes that could have potentially harmful consequences to both the student and the coach. It goes without saying that sexual, intimate, or physical relationships between coach and student athlete is strictly prohibited, regardless of the age of the student. Below are some additional rules and guidelines designed to protect both students and coaches:
  - Personal contact. Contact for social or personal reasons not related to the athletic relationship is highly discouraged. Telephone or e-mail contact with students is also highly discouraged. Coaches should make it a practice to conduct team business during practice or competition. If necessary, communications with the student should be limited to specific school or team issues or team communication (i.e., game cancellation, practice time change, etc.), and the coach should direct their call or e-mail to the parent. Always be sure to avoid comments or conversation of a personal nature when speaking with a student athlete over the phone or via e-mail.
  - Driving student's home. It is never okay to drive a student home unless it is an absolute emergency. Instead, call a parent or guardian. In an emergency, find another adult to ride with you if possible. If no one else is available and you must drive a student home, be sure to inform your supervisor the following day.
  - Locker room safeguards. A male coach should not enter the girls' locker room when female students are present. Likewise, a female coach should not enter the boys' locker room when male students are present. In the event of an emergency, try to find an adult of the opposite sex to accompany you, and always make sure the student athletes are properly dressed/covered before entering.
  - Team social events. All team social events should be approved in advance by the Athletic Director or Principal. If organized and sponsored by the school, the Coach should be the organizer of the event and must include all team members. The purpose and nature of the event should be established with the Athletic Director. Considerations should be made for finances and transportation to

allow all team members the opportunity to attend such events. To avoid ill will among teammates, or allegations of inappropriate behavior, coaches should not be involved in sponsoring, organizing, or hosting a team social event where only part of the team is invited. We also caution coaches about attending a team dinner (or other social event) where only part of the team is invited. Should you choose to attend said events you should make sure that a parent or other responsible adult will also be present, and you should notify the Athletic Director or Administrator in charge of athletics of your attendance at the event as a safeguard. Team overnight events are also highly discouraged. Coaches should be aware of the increased occurrences of hazing that accompany team 'social' events and work to maintain an environment that eliminates such behaviors.

- Open door policy. Whenever speaking to a student, be sure to always do so in a public setting and not behind closed doors. If a student asks to speak with you in private, move away from ear shot of the group, but always be within vision of others whenever possible.
- One-on-one tutoring. If a student requests additional tutoring after practice or competition, try to avoid tutoring one-on-one if possible (i.e., ask another coach to assist you, pair the student up with another athlete on the team who may be able to tutor him/her, etc.) If you need to tutor a student, inform administration and always do so in an open public setting.
- Physical contact. Whereas some physical contact may be an appropriate sign of support or athletic instruction, other times it is not appropriate. Coaches should always be cautious of how their physical contact with students may be interpreted by others, and they should always avoid excessive or inappropriate contact with student athletes (i.e., long affectionate hugs, kissing, slap on the buttocks, etc.).
- Confidant(e). If one of your student athletes is troubled and approaches you for a 'shoulder to lean on,' be aware of the referral process and try to refer the student to other professionals or organizations who may be able to help them. If the student is not comfortable speaking with others, collaborate with the Athletic Director/Administrator with any personal matters the student confides in you. Do not make the decision alone.
- Gestures/Comments. Be aware of how innocent glances, gestures, comments, complements on appearance, or jokes may be interpreted by students or others. Although your intentions may be innocent or even done in kindness, they may backfire if interpreted by others as offensive or inappropriate.

Policies, Rules, and Expectations

Although coaches are responsible for abiding by all (District) policies, procedures, and other rules, we have included a summary of some of these provisions which coaches need to be particularly aware. If you have specific questions about these policies or other (District) policies, please contact the Athletic Director/Administrator of your building. For a complete listing of (District) policies, please visit our website at (District website).

Academic Eligibility

- The (District) recognizes and promotes the priority of academics within the athletic programs. While athletics is an important part of education, academic success remains the primary objective. Coaches are expected to support this position and make every effort to accommodate students' needs as they balance academics with athletics. To emphasize the priority of academics, each school has adopted their own Academic Eligibility regulations. Coaches must have a working knowledge of these regulations and inform both students and parents of these regulations.

Accidents and Injuries

- Accidents are likely to occur from time to time, but preventive measures should keep them to a minimum. Exercise good judgment and care always. Look ahead to possible dangerous consequences, especially in certain areas such as the gymnasium, locker rooms, playing fields, and other areas in which practice or games are held.
- The Athletic Director, Administrator in charge of athletics, or designee must be notified of all student accidents or injuries and a *Student Accident Report* must be completed. When in doubt, notify the Athletic Director anyway.
- If you become injured while coaching, no matter how slight, please be sure to notify the Athletic Director (or Administrator in charge of athletics). If you require medical treatment and/or are unable to work because of the injury, an *Employee's Claim and Employer First Report of Injury* will need to be completed within 24 hours of the injury.

Athletic Equipment and Uniforms

- Ordering equipment. Coaches will comply with school-based practices for ordering equipment and supplies. ALL orders must have *prior* written approval from the Athletic Director (or Administrator in charge of athletics) before they may be ordered. Coaches will be responsible for the payment or return of any equipment/uniforms purchased without prior written approval by the Athletic Director (or Administrator in charge of athletics).
- Care and control of equipment. The coach is responsible for the dispersal and collection, and care and maintenance of all uniforms and equipment used in his/her program. To ensure proper care and control of uniforms and equipment, the coach shall:
  o Establish and maintain a control system to ensure that all uniforms and equipment are accurately accounted for.
  o Instruct team members in the care and use of their uniforms and equipment early in the season and inform players of their responsibility to return all items that are issued to them. A coach who is having difficulty collecting uniforms or equipment from a student at the end of the season should seek assistance from the Athletic Director (or Administrator in charge of athletics).
  o Turn in all uniforms and equipment within 1 week after the last contest of the season. Uniforms should be returned in a clean condition. Equipment is to be

cleaned, stored, and repaired according to manufacturer's instructions. Questions concerning this should be directed to the Athletic Director or Administrator in charge of athletics.
- o Refrain from discarding, selling, or giving away uniforms or equipment without the approval of the Athletic Director (or Administrator in charge of athletics). If approved, disposal of the equipment must be consistent with district policy.

Attendance

- Students must be in school all day to be eligible to practice, compete, or perform, unless the absence is a school-sponsored event or other excused absence. Excused absences must be accompanied by a parent/guardian signed note and approved by the Athletic Director or Principal. Examples of excused absences include doctor's appointments, college visits, etc. The Athletic Director or Principal will review partial attendance or special circumstances.

Communicable Disease

- The district is committed to providing a safe environment for all employees and students. The district also recognizes and respects an individual's right to confidentiality. If you are diagnosed with a contagious disease that may jeopardize the safety of the students and staff (or put them at risk of exposure), please notify the Athletic Director (or Administrator in charge of athletics) in a timely manner so the district can implement the necessary safety precautions if deemed appropriate. Your identity shall remain confidential except as required by Department of Public Health regulations or as necessary to implement district procedures.

Confidentiality

- Coaches are expected to maintain confidentiality of all student records and information in accordance with the Family Educational Rights and Privacy Act of 1974 and the district policy on student records. Coaches should refrain from discussing a student by name unless it is with another school official with a "need to know" the information such as classroom teacher, principal, nurse, special educator, or guidance counselor. Confidentiality should be maintained for all students including regular and special education. If you know many students and their families, you risk slipping from "coach" to "neighbor" role without realizing it. Your rule of thumb should be, "Never discuss specifics of your coaching work outside of school." If you have a concern about any aspect of the athletic program or student athlete, you should take it up directly with the Athletic Director (or Administrator in charge of athletics).

Corporal Punishment and Physical Restraint

- Physical force is not an acceptable means of correction or communication and is against district policy. Physical restraint is authorized only when needed to protect the safety of the individual student, self, and/or other students and employees.

Discipline

- Coaches are expected to follow and support the school-based discipline policy. School-based discipline may result in athletics related consequences at the discretion of the Athletic Director or Administrator in charge of athletics. For example, any student who is suspended or sent to the in-house suspension room or the time out room for disciplinary reasons will not participate in any competitions or practices on that day. Head coaches must have their set of rules specific for their program submitted and approved by the athletic director prior to implementation.

Fire Drill/Emergency Plan

- Each school has an Emergency Plan and established fire/emergency preparedness drills. Coaches must be familiar with the Emergency Plan and fire/emergency preparedness drill instructions at his or her school and are responsible for reviewing the evacuation procedures with all team members. Fire/emergency preparedness drill instructions are posted near each classroom door and the gymnasium. The emergency signal is a continuous loud tone. The recall signal, which allows individuals to reenter the building, shall be established by each school and shall be clearly distinct from any other signal. The coach must be familiar with the signal at their school.
- During fire or emergency preparedness drills, or in the event of an actual emergency, coaches are expected to:
  - Stay with his or her team
  - Take an attendance sheet/roster with them outside
  - Supervise and maintain order
  - Remind students where to meet outside
  - Close all windows in his or her immediate area
  - Assist any student who needs help
  - If activity is held in the gymnasium, close, but do not lock, the gymnasium
  - Take attendance outside

First Aid and Medical Treatment

- All coaches are expected to have up-to-date certifications in first aid and Bloodborne Pathogens Training (BloodbornePathogenTraining.com, 2019).
- Coaches are expected to collect and compile emergency contact information for each team member. Coaches must always carry the emergency contact information for all team members with them (games & practices). Emergency contact information must contain a minimum of the following:
  - Name, address, and home phone number of the student athlete.

- Name(s), address(es), home phone number(s), and emergency phone number(s) of parents and/or guardian(s).
- Name and phone number of family physician or pediatrician.
- Description of the student athlete's special health problem(s).
- Names, addresses, and phone numbers of at least three emergency contact persons authorized to pick up, transport, and make medical decisions related to the student athlete in the event the parents/guardians cannot be reached.
- The coach must be aware of any allergies or special conditions for team members and communicate such to all other coaches who travel with his/her team.
- The coach must have easy access to an emergency medical kit at all games and practices. The medical kit should include ice or ice packs.
- If a player receives an injury that requires first aid and/or additional medical treatment, the coach (or other designee who is certified in first aid) shall provide the necessary first aid, and shall notify the parent/guardian of the injury so that further medical attention can be sought if desired. The coach (or designee) must complete and file a *Student Accident Report* describing the incident and action taken. The injury must also be reported to the Athletic Director, Administrator in charge of athletics, or Athletic Trainer and logged with the school health office the following school day.
- If a player receives an injury that requires emergency medical attention or hospitalization, the coach (or designee) shall contact 911 immediately. If hospitalization is necessary, the player should be transported immediately by private vehicle or ambulance. The coach (or designee) shall immediately contact the parent/guardian or designee after calling 911 and request that they meet the player at the hospital. A staff member or parent/guardian should accompany the athlete if possible. Follow the same reporting procedures as outlined above.
- Any athlete who receives an injury that requires medical treatment beyond first aid must obtain written permission from a doctor before he/she will be allowed to return to participation (practice or competition).
- Coaches are required to follow the directions of the physician to the letter, concerning any treatment and return of the player to participation. It is a good idea for the athlete to ask the physician, during the initial visit, to prescribe a treatment plan for him/her to follow.

Handling Bodily Fluids

- Universal precautions should always be utilized when handling bodily fluids. Whenever possible, direct skin contact with body fluids should be avoided. Disposable gloves should be available in each medical kit and should be used when direct hand contact is anticipated. Dispose of used gloves in a plastic bag or lined trash can. Wash hands thoroughly after any contact with bodily fluids and before contact with others.
- If blood or other potentially infectious materials have contact with broken skin, mucous membrane, or by a bite or needle stick, wash or irrigate the area immediately and report to the school nurse. You will be asked to fill out an

Employee's Claim and Employer First Report of Injury and will be advised to seek immediate medical attention at no cost to you.

Handling of "Sharps"

- Students handling a potentially injurious material or "sharps" require direct supervision. All disposable "sharps" (i.e., razor blades, needles, broken glass, etc.) after use should be placed in biohazard containers provided. Contaminated re-usable "sharps" (i.e., scissors, knifes, tools, etc.) should also immediately be placed into appropriate biohazard containers. These containers are found in the Health Office and in the Science and Practical Arts classrooms and offices of each school.
- If you cannot find an appropriate receptacle, please contact an administrator or custodian immediately. When handling any potentially contaminated or injurious materials protect yourself with disposable gloves. Disposable gloves should be available in each medical kit. If your medical kit does not contain disposable gloves, please notify the Head Coach, Athletic Director, or Administrator in charge of athletics.

Medications

- All student medications are kept in the Health Office and administered by a nurse or under the direction or authorization of the school nurse. Students should be directed to restrain from taking or carrying medications on school premises except as authorized by a doctor, parent, or the school nurse (i.e., epi-pen, insulin, inhaler, etc.). Coaches are not permitted to administer prescription medications, pain medications, or other over-the-counter medications to students except in emergency situations as directed and authorized by the school nurse (i.e., EpiPen injections, insulin, inhaler, etc.).

Insurance

- All candidates for an athletic team are required to furnish proof of accident/health insurance before participating in tryouts, practices, or competitions. The school district does not purchase insurance for its athletes, but the district does offer a school time insurance program at a nominal fee to all enrolled students. Information about the school time insurance may be obtained from the school's main office.

Lightning Standard

- If you hear thunder or see lightning at any time, discontinue practice or game immediately. Activity can resume ½ hour after last heard thunderclap or last seen lightning strike. In any case, use conservative discretion. The safest place is in one of the buildings; dugouts can do when immediate cover is necessary but are not preferred. The training department will be responsible for determining play, delay, or suspension of contests. In association with head coaches, they will cooperate with game officials about cancellation.

Non-Discrimination

- The district policy prohibits discrimination on the basis of disability, marital status, national origin, race, color, religion, age, sex or sexual orientation, or any other protected class as defined by law (Civil Rights Act, 1964).

Hazing

- Hazing is a form of harassment and will not be tolerated in conjunction with any (District) athletic/activities program. Hazing is defined as "any intentional, knowing, and reckless act occurring on or off school grounds, directed against a player or prospective member of a school-sponsored team or group, that endangers the mental or physical health or safety of a student" for the purpose of initiation, admission into, or continued membership of any such team or group (Garland ISD, 2020, pp. 66–67).

  If a student is in violation of *hazing*, consequences may range from individual suspension from participation in the athletic/activities program for a period of time to cancellation of an athletic schedule, depending upon the magnitude of the incident and number of students involved. Consequences for hazing violations brought to the attention of the administration after the season may be applied to and/or include subsequent athletic/activities participation, athletic letter awards, or athletic/activities probation. The athletic/activities director and principal will determine consequences. There is also Texas law making hazing a crime, and students should be aware that, in addition to the school penalties outlined above, they could face prosecution for engaging in hazing (Texas Education Code, 2017b, Sec. 37.152).

- Hazing prevention workshop. Coaches will conduct a hazing prevention workshop with their teams after the start of the season but prior to the first game/competition, and will be required to submit to the Athletic Director (or Administrator in charge of athletics) in writing including names of attendees, materials reviewed, and date(s) of training. Coaches shall educate their teams on the (District) Hazing policy and procedures.

Parent Meeting

- Each head coach is responsible for holding a preseason parent meeting. This can be done by individual team or by sport. Coaches must inform the Athletic Director or Administrator in charge of athletics where and when the meeting will take place, but the meeting must occur before the first official contest of the season. Alternative means of formal communication to parents may also suffice with approval from the Athletic Director (or Administrator in charge of athletics). A copy of the written notice distributed to parents must be provided to the Athletic Director (or Administrator in charge of athletics).

Fundraising

- All fundraising events and use of such funds must be approved in advance by the Athletic Director or Administrator in charge of athletics. All head coaches are expected to participate with athletic department fundraising goals and objectives.

Physical and Health Questionnaire

- Students cannot practice or participate on a school athletic team unless the student provides evidence that she or he has had a physical within the past 2 years and the student's guardian has completed and submitted a health questionnaire (UIL, 2020d).

Political Freedom

- The district shall in no way infringe upon individuals' rights and freedoms of political involvement. However, employees and volunteers of the district must not misuse their position in the school to influence the academic process in the interest of their own political ambitions or those of a political group. Employees, volunteers, and other citizens of the district will not engage in political activity on school premises during school hours.

Reporting Child Abuse and Neglect

- Under Texas law and (District) policy, any school employee who reasonably suspects that a child has been abused or neglected shall report the same to the appropriate law enforcement authorities within 24 hours (Texas Education Agency, 2019). If possible, you should speak directly to the Athletic Director, school administrator, the school's Child Protection Team, or other designee in advance of reporting the abuse/neglect. However, as a mandated reporter, you are obligated to report suspected abuse or neglect regardless to whether the Athletic Director, school administrator, the school's Child Protection Team, or other designee agrees to such. Below is the contact information necessary for proper reporting:

- Call the Department of Family and Protective Services (DFPS) at 1-800-252-5400 (make a written notation of whom the report was made to and when the report was made) and

- Follow up with a written report which can be done online at the Texas Abuse Hotline website: https://www.txabusehotline.org/Login/Default.aspx

Season Summary

- Each coach will be required to submit to the Athletic Director (or Administrator in charge of athletics), within 15-calendar days of the last contest, a summary of the season which should include the following items:

- o Summary of the season including your schedule and scores (high school only) of all contests.
- o Head coaches will submit a written evaluation of each assistant. It is suggested that you go over these evaluations with each assistant, so they clearly understand their strengths and weaknesses.
- o List of award winners so they can be filed and checked for proper award items for each athlete awarded.
- o Turn in all keys if not needed for the following season.
- o Indicate whether it is your current intention to return in the same coaching position for the following school year. This would not constitute a binding obligation on your part or on the school's part, but it would serve the Athletic Director (or Administrator in charge of athletics) for planning purposes.
- o All coaches should take inventory. The forms should be placed on file in the Athletic/school office.
- o Distribute, collect, and review Student Rating Form from each team member.
- o Complete required evaluation form(s) (i.e., self-evaluation, and JV/Frosh/Assistant Coach evaluations for Head Coach) and schedule meeting with Athletic Director or Administrator in charge of athletics.

Team Events

- The district believes team events are a great way to build teamwork, boost spirit, and to recognize accomplishments of student athletes, however, with any team event comes potential for liability and an opportunity for misconduct if not properly organized and supervised. As such, coaches must receive pre-approval for hosting, planning, or taking part in any team event outside of practice or competitions. Requests must be received in writing and show when and where the event will take place, and the names of other chaperones that will be in attendance. Consideration must be given to cost, location, travel, and timing of events to ensure that all team members have an opportunity to attend the event. Coaches are responsible to report knowledge of any student athlete misconduct that occurs during an official or non-official team event, whether the coach attends the event.

Tobacco, Vaping, and Substance Abuse

- Tobacco use, vaping, possession, or distribution is not permitted in any school building or on school grounds at any time. Being under the influence of, possessing, using, or distributing alcohol, marijuana, or drugs in school, on school property or during a school sponsored event is strictly prohibited. Any student violation should be reported to the Athletic Director or Administrator in charge of athletics. If you observe any student who appears to have a substance abuse problem, or if a concerned informant or friend alerts you, you should refer the situation to the Athletic Director or school administrator. While it is human nature to try to help and express your concern, just as in child abuse/neglect situations, trained professionals must be the ones to deal with the situation.

Training Rules

- To help promote a healthy lifestyle, responsible behavior, and optimal team and individual performance in our students, the district maintains and enforces a "zero tolerance policy" with respect to violations of the training rules. Coaches shall inform students of the training rules and play a key role in enforcing these rules.
- A coach who becomes aware of any violation(s) of the training rule, must notify the Athletic Director (or Administrator in charge of athletics) promptly.

Transportation

- Coaches are responsible for supervising the transportation of students to and from athletic events and ensuring compliance with district policy. Whenever a school vehicle, chartered vehicle, or rented vehicle is used for the transportation of students to an athletic contest, all students are to travel to and from the contest with the team. Exceptions must be requested in writing by a parent and must be approved by the athletic/activities director or coach/advisor. Only parents or other responsible designated adults may provide transportation, and under no circumstances will a student be permitted to ride with another student or drive him/herself to any athletic event (this provision applies even if the student driver is 18 years of age or older). While on the bus, students are expected to adhere to the rules of the driver and bus leasing agency.

Transporting Students

- Coaches are not allowed to drive students home (or elsewhere) except in the case of an emergency. In an emergency, the coach shall find another adult to ride with him or her if possible. If no one else is available and the student must be driven home (or elsewhere), the coach must inform his or her supervisor the following day.

Travel and Away Games

- Coaches are solely responsible for the supervision of team members while visiting and traveling to and from other schools. Students are to be reminded that they are representing their school at all away games or events, and they are expected to demonstrate good judgment, respect, and high moral. In this light, coaches should recommend students dress in an appropriate manner when traveling. It is imperative that the coach is the last individual from the school to leave the locker room of the host school. Locker rooms should be left neat and orderly. Should damage arise or incidents occur, the Athletic Director or Administrator in charge of athletics should be notified of the situation as soon as possible.

Unlawful Harassment

- It is the policy of the district to maintain a learning and working environment that is free from unlawful harassment. The district prohibits any form of unlawful harassment based on disability, marital status, national origin, race, color, religion, age, sex, or sexual orientation (Civil Rights Act, 1964). Unlawful harassment includes verbal or physical conduct which has the purpose or effect of substantially interfering with a person's performance or creating an intimidating, hostile, or offensive environment. *Sexual harassment* is a form of unlawful harassment, which consists of unwelcome sexual advances, requests for sexual favors, and other verbal or physical conduct or communication of a sexual nature (United Nations, 1992). You should report any instance of harassment or violence to the principal who will see that it is investigated according to district policy.

Volunteers

- The district believes volunteers can be a benefit to both student athletes and coaches and are essential to the success of our schools. Volunteers offer special skills and abilities, which enhance and supplement the athletic program, and we encourage every opportunity for productive partnerships with all constituents of the community. Before an individual performs duties as a volunteer within our athletic programs, she or he must be approved by the Athletic Director (or Administrator in charge of athletics), and properly registered with the school. All approved volunteers must also sign a *Volunteer Agreement* annually. If you plan to use other individuals to assist you in your program, please be sure to notify the Athletic Director (or Administrator in charge of athletics). The UIL has strict rules on volunteers. Before allowing any volunteers, all must be approved prior to assisting the program.
- Coaches are responsible for supervising volunteers and to be sure they adhere to the Professional Standards of Conduct, Policies and Procedures, and Other General Rules & Expectations outlined in the Coaches Guide.

Weapons and Fireworks

- In conformance with federal and state law, possession of firearms, fireworks, or other weapons is strictly prohibited unless permitted. Any student violation should be reported to the Athletic Director or school administrator immediately.

Training Requirements

- All coaches are expected to minimally meet the training requirements as outlined by the UIL. For information about training requirements and other available training, please visit the district website at (District website).
- All coaches are also required to complete the Concussion in Sports training. One source of this training is the National Federation of State High School Associations (2020).

Abiding by District Policies

- All coaches are expected to adhere to the district policies as they apply to coaches. District policies can be found at (District website).
- Demonstrate how to share athletes with other sports.
- Demonstrate how to share facilities with other coaches.

- Demonstrate effective communication with students and parents.
- Develop an enforceable parent/coach communication policy
- Coaches realize and nurture the talent in other colleagues and students.

Align and Organize Athletic Department

- Organize and maintain chain of command procedures.
- Follow complaint procedure: write concern and solution and have meeting set at most appropriate level. Exhaust all steps. If not resolved, then file Level 1 complaint through athletic secretary office.
- Athletic Director conduct pre-season and post-season head coach evaluations.

Conduct Pre-Season and Post-Season Evaluations

This is a time the athletic director and each head coach will visit about the expectations of the season (pre-season) or results of the season (post-season). Have the coach evaluate themselves prior to the meeting.

Athletic Director and Head Coach Evaluation(s)

Example of Coach Evaluation Record

EMPLOYEE NAME _____ CAMPUS _____

POSITION/SPORT COACHED_____ DATE _____

P = PROFICIENT; NI = NEEDS IMPROVEMENT; U = UNACCEPTABLE; N/A = NOT APPLICABLE

I. PROFESSIONAL AND PERSONAL RELATIONSHIP

	P	NI	U	NA
1. Maintains open lines of communication with campus administration both verbally and in writing; regularly updates administration and athletic director regarding athletic issues.	☐	☐	☐	☐
2. Provides written teach rules, as approved by campus principal, to squad members and parents.	☐	☐	☐	☐
3. Employs fair and consistent behavior management strategies for all student athletes; heeds due process procedures when investigating student/team misconduct.	☐	☐	☐	☐
4. Dresses appropriately at practices and games.	☐	☐	☐	☐
5. Develops effective public relations with the school, parents, and community.	☐	☐	☐	☐
6. Supports student athletes/athletic program by participating in sports related school functions.	☐	☐	☐	☐
7. Maintains appropriate professional conduct towards players, coaches, officials, and patrons at athletic practices and games.	☐	☐	☐	☐
8. Works cooperatively with coaches at the middle school and high school levels to develop a coordinated, comprehensive, and vertically aligned athletic programs.	☐	☐	☐	☐
9. Promotes all sports in the athletic program and fosters school spirit and price.	☐	☐	☐	☐

10. Establishes and maintains open lines of communication with students and parents. ☐ ☐ ☐ ☐

11. Works cooperatively with coaching staff. ☐ ☐ ☐ ☐

12. Works cooperatively with campus administration. ☐ ☐ ☐ ☐

13. Works cooperatively with Athletic Department. ☐ ☐ ☐ ☐

Comments/Commendations:

_____

_____

_____

II. COACHING PERFORMANCE

2. Models respect for athletes, coaches, officials, and patrons during all coaching situations and athletic events. ☐ ☐ ☐ ☐

3. Provides responsible supervision for student athletes. ☐ ☐ ☐ ☐

4. Demonstrates knowledge and expertise in his/her sport. ☐ ☐ ☐ ☐

5. Develops and implements effective leadership strategies that foster individual and team success. ☐ ☐ ☐ ☐

6. Designs flexible, well-coordinated and well-organized practice/game schedules that maximize teach, staff, and facility resources. ☐ ☐ ☐ ☐

7. Models the fundamental philosophy, skills, and techniques endorsed by the XISD Athletic Department for student athletes. ☐ ☐ ☐ ☐

8. Demonstrates respect and good sportsmanship on and off the playing field, establishes expectations for student athletes and staff to do the same. ☐ ☐ ☐ ☐

9. Updates coaching techniques and ideas. ☐ ☐ ☐ ☐

10. Models effective leadership skills that promote positive attitudes and efforts among student athletes. ☐ ☐ ☐ ☐

11. Follows required guidelines for addressing student injuries as found in the Athletic Handbook, board policy, and district procedures. ☐ ☐ ☐ ☐

12. Delegates responsibility to assistant coaches while maintaining full responsibility for the program and sport (head coaches only). ☐ ☐ ☐ ☐

13. Uses effective, appropriate motivational strategies that comply with the Educators Code of Ethics for teachers and coaches, board policy, and athletic department requirements. ☐ ☐ ☐ ☐

14. Places appropriate emphasis on the role of competitive athletics in the total development of the student athlete. ☐ ☐ ☐ ☐

15. Communicates to student athletes the importance of accepting responsibility for their own decisions and behavior in and outside athletics. ☐ ☐ ☐ ☐

16. Utilizes effective scouting methods and techniques to improve team's performance. ☐ ☐ ☐ ☐

17. Achieves optimal individual and/or team performance levels that extend beyond season win-loss records. ☐ ☐ ☐ ☐

Comments/Commendations:

_____

_____

_____

III. RELATED COACHING RESPONSIBILITIES

1. Actively participates in campus initiatives which address academic success. ☐ ☐ ☐ ☐

2. Ensures all student athletes meet eligibility requirements in accordance with UIL competition guidelines. ☐ ☐ ☐ ☐

3. Encourages athletes to participate in as many sports as desired. ☐ ☐ ☐ ☐

4. Supports student athletes' participation in other school related activities. ☐ ☐ ☐ ☐

5. Encourages and/or facilitates opportunities for athletes to further develop individual and teach skills during pre- and post-season periods (high school only). ☐ ☐ ☐ ☐

6. Demonstrates a willingness to share athletic facilities with other school related programs. ☐ ☐ ☐ ☐

7. Attends in-services, athletic department/school meetings and sports clinics necessary for the growth of the athletic program and the improvement of coaching performance. ☐ ☐ ☐ ☐

8. Attends all meetings, practices, and athletic events at designated times. ☐ ☐ ☐ ☐

9. Follows requirements as described in the Athletic Handbook, board policy, and district procedures. ☐ ☐ ☐ ☐

10. Understand and follows rules and regulations set forth by all governing agencies, including but not limited to UIL, TEA, XISD Board of Trustees, the District, professional organizations, and campus administration. ☐ ☐ ☐ ☐

11. Submits required documents as listed in the Athletic Handbook to the campus and Athletic Department in a timely manner. ☐ ☐ ☐ ☐

12. Provides a written report to campus administration and the Athletic Department regarding any critical incident as soon as practical, and no later than 24 hours after the incident, unless otherwise required by the school principal or the Athletic Department. ☐ ☐ ☐ ☐

13. Assumes responsibility for the proper procurement and care of athletic equipment. ☐ ☐ ☐ ☐

14. Maintains and prepares facilities and equipment for practice and competition in accordance with athletic department, board policy, and district procedures. ☐ ☐ ☐ ☐

15. Follows district guidelines for the purchase of equipment as specified in the Athletic Handbook, board policy, and district procedures. ☐ ☐ ☐ ☐

Comments/Commendations:

_____

_____

_____

IV. SUPERVISION/LEADERSHIP

(The criteria in this Domain apply to Athletic Coordinators only)

1. Serves as a liaison for the Athletic Department. ☐ ☐ ☐ ☐

2. Communicates Athletic Department information and philosophy via monthly and regularly schedule coaches' meetings. ☐ ☐ ☐ ☐

3. Works collaboratively with male/female head coaches to address issues related to the campus athletic program. ☐ ☐ ☐ ☐

4. Assists in the selection and hiring of new coaches. ☐ ☐ ☐ ☐

5. Assists in the evaluation of campus-based coaches. ☐ ☐ ☐ ☐

6. Supervises and coordinates campus athletic facilities. ☐ ☐ ☐ ☐

7. Monitors and maintains up-to-date records for the assigned athletic programs. ☐ ☐ ☐ ☐

8. Uses 5 Measure Report Card data to provide support, guidance, and direction to coaches regarding the athletic program. ☐ ☐ ☐ ☐

Comments/Commendations:

_____

_____

_____

☐   I have read this performance review and I agree with its content.

☐   I have read this performance review and I do not agree with its content.

Response will follow: ☐ YES   ☐ NO

SIGNATURES:

EMPLOYEE: _____ DATE: _____
(Name & Title)

CAMPUS ADMINISTRATOR: _____ DATE: _____
(Name & Title)

IMPROVE PROFESSIONAL AND PERSONAL RELATIONSHIPS

1. Maintains open lines of communication with campus administration both verbally and in writing; regularly updates administration and athletic coordinator regarding athletic issues.

   PERFORMANCE DESCRIPTOR: Meets with administrators on a regular basis or as needed, shares coordinator agendas with appropriate staff, and reports issues of concern to designated individual (s) in a timely manner.

2. Provides written team rules, as approved by campus principal, to squad members and parents.

   PERFORMANCE DESCRIPTOR: Maintains filed copies of current team rules that have been approved by the campus principal and signed by student athletes and parents.

3. Employs fair and consistent behavior management strategies with all student athletes and heeds due process procedures when investigating student/team misconduct.

   PERFORMANCE DESCRIPTOR: Implements a written discipline management plan that is fair, consistent, allows for due process for student athletes, and maintains individual and team discipline in a positive manner. Teams' rules should be clearly defined and include a progression of consequences from verbal/written warnings, coach/team discipline, parent notification, suspension, or, in extreme cases, removal from team. Specific rules should reference behavior consequences for unexcused absences from school and/or games, tardiness, un-sportsmanship-like behavior, and violating the student code of conduct. Major infractions such as felonies may result in immediate removal from the team.

4. Dresses appropriately at practices and games as recommended by the Athletic Department and indicated in the Athletic Handbook.

    PERFORMANCE DESCRIPTOR: Exhibits sports-appropriate dress and appearance during athletic practice and game situations. Coaching attire in school colors will be worn at practice. Professional attire in game situations will be sport specific.

5. Develops effective public relations with the school, parents, and the community.

    PERFORMANCE DESCRIPTOR: Develops and maintains good public relations with colleagues, parents, and community. Attends booster club meetings, reports scores and stats to newspapers, holds parent meetings at the beginning of the season, and posts game results on district website.

6. Supports student athletes/athletic program by participating in sports related school functions.

    PERFORMANCE DESCRIPTOR: Shows interest in student athletes' accomplishments on and off the playing field. Attends Parents' Night, sports banquets, athletic awards ceremonies, and pep rally assemblies. Prepares and sends recommendation letters to colleges on behalf of future athletes.

7. Maintains appropriate professional conduct towards players, coaches, officials, and patrons at athletic practices and games.

    PERFORMANCE DESCRIPTOR: Demonstrates diplomacy, tact, self-control, and respect for all.

8. Works cooperatively with coaches at the elementary, middle school, and high school levels to develop a coordinated, comprehensive, and vertically aligned athletic program.

    PERFORMANCE DESCRIPTOR: Works with cluster coaches at every level to develop well-coordinated, vertically aligned athletic programs by visiting area campuses, and observing athletic practices and games. Coaches are expected to run the same offensive and defensive schemes/systems throughout the cluster in appropriate sports.

9. Promotes all sports in the athletic program and fosters school spirit and pride.

PERFORMANCE DESCRIPTOR: Provides leadership in the development and implementation of the total campus athletic program and promotes positive staff morale, attitudes, and enthusiasm.

10. Establishes and maintains open lines of communication with students and parents.

PERFORMANCE DESCRIPTOR: Organizes and prepares pre-season meetings with parents to review team policies, procedures, calendar, and additional information regarding the upcoming sports season. Conducts parent/coach conferences as needed.

11. Works cooperatively with coaching staff.

PERFORMANCE DESCRIPTOR: Accepts and acts upon constructive criticism in a professional manner. Develops loyalty, flexibility, and a spirit of cooperation among colleagues, campus administration, and Athletic Department.

12. Works cooperatively with campus administration.

PERFORMANCE DESCRIPTOR: Accepts and acts upon constructive criticism in a professional manner. Develops loyalty, flexibility, and a spirit of cooperation among colleagues, campus administration, and Athletic Department.

13. Works cooperatively with the Athletic Department.

PERFORMANCE DESCRIPTOR: Accepts and acts upon constructive criticism in a professional manner. Develops loyalty, flexibility and a spirit of cooperation among colleagues, campus administration and athletic department.

V. COACHING PERFORMANCE

1. Models respect for athletes, coaches, officials, and patrons during all coaching situations and athletic events.

PERFORMANCE DESCRIPTOR: Acts as a role model for athletes by exhibiting integrity, dependability, emotional stability, and maturity. Demonstrates fairness and patience with team members. Provides constructive criticism and is generous with praise. Teaches respect for officials and their decisions. Exhibits appropriate dress code and appearance.

2. Provides responsible supervision for student athletes.

PERFORMANCE DESCRIPTOR: Provides effective team supervision on and off campus grounds before, during, and after practices and games.

3. Demonstrates knowledge and expertise in his or her sport.

    PERFORMANCE DESCRIPTOR: Makes good decisions during game situations and teaches fundamental skills and appropriate drills.

4. Develops and implements effective leadership strategies that foster individual and team success.

    PERFORMANCE DESCRIPTOR: Develops written rules and procedures for student athletes. Always motivates players to give maximum effort. Coaches all players. Encourages the development of strong, positive, and competitive attitudes among players.

5. Designs flexible, well-coordinated, and well-organized practice/game schedules that maximize team, staff, and facility resources.

    PERFORMANCE DESCRIPTOR: Organizes and prepares for daily practices. Organizes and develops creative game plans and weekly itineraries. Efficiently delegates responsibility to assistant coaches. Plans and executes programs to achieve short- and long-term goals.

6. Models the fundamental philosophy, skills, and techniques endorsed by the XISD Athletic Department for student athletes.

    PERFORMANCE DESCRIPTOR: Keeps current with, demonstrates knowledge of, and adheres to XISD Athletic Department, board, and district policies.

7. Demonstrates respect and good sportsmanship on and off the playing field and establishes expectations for student athletes and staff to do the same.

    PERFORMANCE DESCRIPTOR: Encourages positive interactions and good sportsmanship between athletes and opponents. Enforces a "no taunting" policy and teaches/models respect for officials and their decisions.

8. Updates coaching techniques and ideas.

    PERFORMANCE DESCRIPTOR: Keeps abreast of and utilizes new and innovative concepts, ideas, and current technology through clinics, reading material, observation of competitors, and other teams, shares ideas with colleagues and peers. Maintains involvement in professional organizations.

9. Models effective leadership skills that promote positive attitudes and efforts among student athletes.

    PERFORMANCE DESCRIPTOR: Exhibits positive attitude and enthusiasm.

10. Follows required guidelines for addressing student injuries as found in the Athletic Handbook, board policy, and district procedures.

    PERFORMANCE DESCRIPTOR: Self-explanatory.

11. Delegates responsibility to assistant coaches while maintaining full responsibility for the program or sport (Head Coaches only).

    PERFORMANCE DESCRIPTOR: Self-explanatory.

12. Uses effective and appropriate motivational strategies that comply with the Educators Code of Ethics for teachers and coaches, board policy, and athletic department requirements.

    PERFORMANCE DESCRIPTOR: Provides recognition of athletes' accomplishments. Promotes positive team morale. Always motivates players to give maximum effort using strategies such as pre-game and half-time pep talks.

13. Places appropriate emphasis on the role of competitive athletics in the total development of the student athlete.

    PERFORMANCE DESCRIPTOR: Involves all athletes in team concepts, promoting growth of character in student athletes.

14. Communicates to student athletes the importance of accepting responsibility for their own decisions and behavior in and outside athletics.

    PERFORMANCE DESCRIPTOR: Maintains individual and team discipline in a fair and positive manner. Enforces team rules consistently. Notifies parents, athletic coordinator, and campus administrators when extreme discipline (such as dismissal) is required.

15. Utilizes effective scouting methods and techniques to improve team's performance.

    PERFORMANCE DESCRIPTOR: Assign scouts, uses and interprets scouting reports, and incorporates the information gained into game plans.

16. Achieves optimal individual and/or team performance levels that extend beyond season win-loss records.

    PERFORMANCE DESCRIPTOR: Athletes demonstrate correct fundamental skills, have good attitudes, demonstrate teamwork, exhibit high levels of competitiveness, and participate in organized, consistent practices. Coaches can maintain and increase student athlete participation in their sports programs.

VI. RELATED COACHING RESPONSIBILITIES

1. Actively participates in campus initiatives which address academic success.

    PERFORMANCE DESCRIPTOR: Shows interest in the classroom endeavors of student athletes. Initiates study hall and tutoring sessions, supports campus efforts and initiatives, encourages student participation in Saturday School, and consistently monitors students' academic progress. Establishes and maintains appropriate coach/student athlete relationship.

2. Ensures all student athletes meet eligibility requirements in accordance with UIL competition guidelines.

    PERFORMANCE DESCRIPTOR: Demonstrates promptness and efficiency with clerical work related to student athlete eligibility: physicals, parent approval, insurance, transfers, end-of-season reports, academic eligibility, equipment, inventories, etc.

3. Encourages athletes to participate in as many sports as desired.

    PERFORMANCE DESCRIPTOR: Facilitates complaints from parents and or students regarding coaches' pressuring athletes to participate in a particular sport. Coordinates opportunities for coaches of other sports to invite athletes to participate in their sport; allows athletes to go to off-season programs in a fair manner.

4. Supports student athletes' participation in other school related activities.

    PERFORMANCE DESCRIPTOR: Supports participation in other sports and school activities of interest to the student athlete: band, fine arts, student council, PALS, ROTC, etc. Makes an effort to attend students' activities and works with other club sponsors to allow adequate practice time among shared activities.

5. Encourages and/or facilitates opportunities for athletes to further develop individual and team skills during pre- and post-season periods.

    PERFORMANCE DESCRIPTOR: Opens gym and weight room during off-season, holiday, and summer periods; encourages year-long, sport-specific conditioning programs. Provides information related to summer sports leagues and tournament opportunities.

6. Demonstrates a willingness to share athletic facilities with other school-related programs.

    PERFORMANCE DESCRIPTOR: Aids in promoting effective school and public relations by sharing athletic facilities for faculty/student athletic competitions;

offers the gymnasium for large group activities; allows for community education classes, fitness and health-related activities in athletic areas, track, etc.

7. Attends in-services, athletic department/school meetings, and sports clinics necessary for the growth of the athletic program and the improvement of coaching performance.

PERFORMANCE DESCRIPTOR: Engages in continuous professional improvement and learning as provided by the XISD. Attends booster club meetings, reports scores and stats to newspapers, holds parent meetings at the beginning of the season, and posts game results on the district website.

8. Attends all meetings, practices, and athletic events at designated times.

PERFORMANCE DESCRIPTOR: Self-explanatory

9. Follows requirements as described in the Athletic Handbook, board policy, and district procedures.

PERFORMANCE DESCRIPTOR: Self-explanatory

10. Understands and follows rules and regulations set forth by all governing agencies, including but not limited to UIL, TEA, XISD Board of Trustees, the District, professional organizations, and campus administration.

PERFORMANCE DESCRIPTOR: Self-explanatory

11. Submits required documents as listed in the Athletic Handbook to the campus and Athletic Department in a timely manner.

PERFORMANCE DESCRIPTOR: Self-explanatory

12. Provides a written report to campus administration and the Athletic Department regarding any critical incident as soon as practical, and not later than 24 hours after the incident, unless otherwise required by the school principal or the Athletic Department.

PERFORMANCE DESCRIPTOR: Critical incidents must be reported to the campus principal and Athletic Department within 24 hours of occurrence; emergency situations must immediately be reported by phone to the school principal. An explanation of specific critical incidents can be found in the XISD Athletic Department Handbook.

13. Assumes responsibility for the proper procurement and care of athletic equipment.

PERFORMANCE DESCRIPTOR: Organizes the effective issuance and collection of athletic equipment; plans for the efficient purchasing, storage, and security of equipment. Inspects and maintains equipment to ensure student safety. Purchases, stores, and secures equipment as per district, athletic department, and campus guidelines.

14. Maintains and prepares facilities and equipment for practice and competition in accordance with the Athletic Department, board policy, and district procedures.

PERFORMANCE DESCRIPTOR: Maintains district's standards of game uniforms. Supervises and maintains cleanliness of weight rooms, dressing rooms, and athletic facilities

15. Follows district guidelines for the purchase of equipment as specified in the Athletic Handbook, board policy, and district procedures.

PERFORMANCE DESCRIPTOR: Self-explanatory

VII. SUPERVISION/LEADERSHIP

1. Serves as a liaison for the Athletic Department.

PERFORMANCE DESCRIPTOR: Addresses concerns and issues with school administration, athletic office, coaches, athletes, parents, booster organizations, community, etc.

2. Communicates athletic department information and philosophy via monthly and regularly scheduled coaches' meetings.

PERFORMANCE DESCRIPTOR: Provides staff agendas at monthly meetings; disseminates information received at coordinator's meetings to athletic staff.

3. Works collaboratively with male and/or female head coaches to address issues related to the campus athletic program.

PERFORMANCE DESCRIPTOR: Supervises staff effectively and promotes staff development. Meets regularly with coaches and promotes positive staff morale. Engages in shared decision-making processes. Maintains consistency between male and female athletic programs.

4. Develops a collaborative and vertically aligned program for campuses with their middle school feeders.

PERFORMANCE DESCRIPTOR: Relays expectations to staff; monitors practices and games; provides positive feedback and constructive criticism to coaches about observed practices and games; utilizes observation and verbal counseling reports; provides guidance to improve performance; facilitates training among cluster coaches regarding standard team plays, game, and sports strategies.

5. Assists in the selection and hiring of new coaches.

   PERFORMANCE DESCRIPTOR: Provides input to campus administrators and Athletic Department regarding the selection and hiring of new coaches, including a review of resumes, job search, interviews, and final selection.

6. Assists in the evaluation of campus-based coaches.

   PERFORMANCE DESCRIPTOR: Assists campus administration with the evaluation of campus-based coaches including the completion of evaluation records as appropriate. Provides formal and informal input to coaches and administrators through observations of practices and competitions. Uses documentation tools to provide positive feedback and constructive criticism. Performs coach/staff evaluations efficiently and in a timely manner.

7. Supervises and coordinates campus athletic facilities.

   PERFORMANCE DESCRIPTOR: Ensures that campus facilities are utilized fairly by all staff and community.

8. Monitors and maintains up-to-date records for the assigned athletic programs.

   PERFORMANCE DESCRIPTOR: Demonstrates effective organization and management skills. Exhibits effective oral and written communication skills. Maintains squad lists, insurance forms, squad size forms, end-of-season reports, win-loss records, physicals, parent approvals, eligibility lists, and letterman procedures.

9. Collects and inputs data each 9 weeks.

   PERFORMANCE DESCRIPTOR: Disaggregates data and analyzes reports. Meets with head coaches regarding data. Uses data to inform decisions regarding the athletic program.

Note. Performance Descriptors are intended to serve as an example of performance expectations for coaches. This list is by no means exhaustive. Additional criteria may apply.

CHAPTER EIGHT:
Moving Forward

Support Athletics Mission, Be A Team Member, and Serve Assigned Athletic Duties for the Program: Committees, Sport Assignments, Organizing Sport Spirit Projects/Groups

Athletic directors should not only be willing but anxious to join other committees, sport assignments, and organize sport spirit projects/groups. This incorporates the team model. As in the book *Good to Great* (Collins, 2001), be a humble, servant leader.

Develop a Youth Spirit Group: Bleacher Creatures

A major addition to any athletic department is to include the youth of the community. Create a youth program to include elementary students. Programs such as the "Bleacher Creatures" will promote games, increase attendance, and develop loyal ties to your program.

It will be imperative to provide information and instructions.

Example of "Bleacher Creature" instructions for elementary students, Grades 1-6, in your local community.

- Get the bleacher creature form updated and then signed by the superintendent.
- Make copies for all elementary schools in the district and the junior highs.
- Grades 1-6 can participate in bleacher creatures.
- Students lead the football team to victory by running out on the field at home games several minutes before the team arrives to the field. They run to the 50-yard line and back to where they began (inflatable helmet, if available).
- If parents purchased tickets for the game that night, they would pick up their bleacher creature in front of a designated location and proceed to the bleachers. Children will not be released until someone is there to pick them up. If parents are not attending the game, they can pick up their bleacher creature at the same gate (designated area) they had dropped them off.
- Students can arrive at the holding area 1 hour prior to kickoff. This allows time to line them up and get them ready to run.
- After parents fill out a form and pays for a ticket for each game, the bleacher creature can run at every home game through the football season.
- The student must have a bleacher creature t-shirt on to be eligible to run at the game. The same t-shirt will be wore for each home game.
- A local t-shirt dealer will provide bleacher creature t-shirts for the school to sell.
- There is a designated drop-off gate, labeled for bleacher creatures.

Support Staff:

1. One Junior High and one JV Blue coach will "corral" the creatures at the south end of the stadium in the fenced waiting area. Creatures report at 7:00 pm to the holding area.
2. The JV cheerleaders will lead the creatures to the inflatable helmet and at the appropriate time (7:10 pm) run with the creatures to the 50-yard line (7:15 pm) then return.
3. Parents will pick up their creatures after the run in the "holding area." Coaches cannot leave until every creature has been united with parent(s).
4. If creature does not have a ticket, they can run out on the field but after the run will not be able to enter the stadium seating. Parent and child will leave.
5. Cheerleaders will assist the younger children. Older creatures will be in front of the line.
6. Creatures for games usually average approximately 400-500 students, so it is very important to have proper assistance from the cheerleaders.
7. Demonstrate an understanding of the need to preserve interscholastic sport in schools as an extension of the classroom where student participants learn important lessons of living a positive, healthy, and productive life.
8. Assign TEAM coordination leadership servant positions.

    Conduct four segment town meeting-seminars. Cover one of the following in each town hall:

    a. Facilities
    b. Athletic Procedures
    c. Sunset Review Committee
    d. Branding
9. Pep Rallies

Promote Importance of Coaches in the Classroom. Add Stipends

This article explains why coaches are important in the educational system.

Welch, J. (2012). *Coaching/teaching stipends: "Best bang for the buck."* THSCA Weekly Headlines. https://www.multibriefs.com/briefs/thsca/thsca022013.pdf

The Texas public school finance system is broken. The Texas Legislature and the U.S. Congress have established higher expectations for public schools while cutting funding. New accountability systems at the federal and state levels impose penalties on schools not meeting academic expectations (Lesley, 2010). The next biennium will have an $8-billion reduction in state funding for public education and force school districts to dip into fund balances, reduce staff, and/or drop programs. Some districts will charge students to participate in extracurricular programs and reduce personnel. The time is now to speak up for coaches and teachers receiving stipends to work in extracurricular programs.

The shortage in school funding requires districts to scrutinize every penny. Therefore, it is so important for administrators and school boards to understand the importance of keeping stipends in place and even consider adding stipends to "exemplary teachers" for additional duties. The "bang for the buck" is the exemplary teacher working extra with students. Extracurricular activities produce high values of life-learned lessons, sportsmanship, and character enhancement. In addition, extracurricular activities further build connections between students and staff.

What is a coach? A coach is a teacher. With only a few exceptions (athletic director, coordinators, or specialist), the coach is a classroom teacher. This person serves the classroom in an academic setting and then works before, during, and after school with students in sports, band, choir, etc. A stipend remunerates for the "extra" work the teacher/coach performs with the students. Stipends paid to teacher/coaches are not proportional to normal salary wages. Considering a full athletic stipend of $6,000-$10,000 and working 20 to 30 hours per week (coaching the sport, bus rides, game time, film evaluation, game planning, staff meetings, etc.), the hours computed for time the teacher/coach works extra, usually does not equal minimum wage. This is a great example of the" bang for the buck."

Research studies provide policy makers with evidence that money well spent improves educational opportunities (Lesley, 2010). Lesley stated the following areas make significant differences in educational outcomes:
- Effective teachers
- Small class sizes
- Rigorous curriculum
- Pre-kindergarten
- Interventions for struggling students

Each of these educational strategies (except pre-kindergarten) prevails in extracurricular activities. Effective teachers work to build connections with students. Small class sizes are prevalent with coaches (position coaches) working in small groups. Rigorous curriculum is teaching the points of the game, game plans, and skill work. Interventions with struggling students are the relationship building coaches do daily in instruction, mentoring, and team building with students. Coaches demonstrate excellence in these areas daily.

Coaching/teaching stipends need to remain intact when districts cut budgets. Administrators need to make sure the employees who work with and teach children in and out of the academic classroom receive priority. Instead of cutting stipends, the need to add stipends is more prevalent now than ever before. The "exemplary" teachers need to be located and offered additional responsibilities of leadership within the district. Lesley (2010) said the most important factor in providing students with opportunities to learn is their access to quality teachers. Scientific studies almost unanimously find that quality teachers lead students to high levels of educational success (Lesley, 2010).

Additional responsibilities and stipends added to exemplary teachers save the district money. It is more cost effective for a district to have eight teachers (doing the work of nine) receiving stipends, rather than nine teachers who do not receive a stipend. When a district adds the ninth teacher, other costs occur such as district payment of health insurance and Texas Teachers Retirement. There is merit to compensating fewer employees. In my opinion, the quality of education and the cost savings to a district improve when exemplary teachers are paid stipends for doing extra work for the district.

Why do certain athletic teams, bands, and choirs, excel every year? We must look at the leadership first. Quality teachers and coaches having proper resources spell success (Dyer, 2010). Working conditions make a huge difference, along with competitive salaries, small class sizes, administrator support, and adequate instructional resources (Lesley, 2010). Quality coaches are quality teachers. Extracurricular activities assist students in excelling academically and physically, increase attendance, lower dropout rates, improve social skills, strengthen character, and promote academic success (no-pass, no-play).

In 2007, economists conducted a research project in California that determined quality teachers raise graduation rates (Levin & Belfield, 2007). Schools attract better teachers through higher salaries and better working conditions. The economists determined raising teacher salaries by 10%, and keeping dropouts in school for two additional years, would cost approximately $82,000 per student. The savings for the public (taxes paid and savings in social services) would be approximately $209,000 for each additional graduate. This would be a net value of $127,000 (Levin & Belfield, 2007). What a return on the investment! School district administrators and boards need to remember the coach/teacher is working "extra" with the students before and after school and receives a small stipend. These teachers have extra duties and the stipends need to remain intact. "Exemplary" teachers should be sought out and offered additional duties, so that students receive that best education funding will provide.

How can a district even consider cutting stipends? It cannot! One of the biggest assets to districts is the teachers who perform extra duties. Many of the "exemplary" teachers could perform other important necessities in educating students before, during, and after school. Quality teachers would be recognized for excellence and receive additional pay. Higher pay and better working conditions ensures retention of the "exemplary" teachers (Levin & Belfield, 2007). Let us encourage school administrators to consider these options if staff cuts are necessary. It would take six to eight stipends to equal one non-teaching salary. Let us keep our exemplary teachers and give our students the best education that district funding can provide. In challenging economic times, we must think outside the box. The state is cutting education and not supporting students with the necessary funding (Lesley, 2010). Speaking up can make a difference.

Develop Student-Athletes

- Develop an enforceable parent/coach communication policy
- Demonstrate conflict mediation with students, parents, and colleagues.
- Study halls (Red-White-Blue)
- Conduct preseason meetings with students and parents.
- Understand your primary role is to make sure the students who participate are safe from potential harm and cared for properly in the event of an injury.

- Be educated about critical issues concerning concussion, hydration, non-abusive environment, and sexual harassment, in conjunction with learning proper tackling procedures and sports strategies.
- Train athletes in the weight room. Strengthening the ligaments and tendons of the joint, while building muscle.
- Goal setting-coaches will encourage and promote "dreaming" and how to build a plan to reach the dream.
- Skills development-coaches will understand and demonstrate how to build trust.

Assist All Head Coaches in Developing Leaders

The athletic director will meet with each head coach and review their plan to develop leadership in their program. Have a model to illustrate what you are looking for in a leadership model. Below is an example. Do not use your example unless the head coach is needing help. They need to develop their own because it will match what they are looking for.

Example:

Create mottos: S (Student) A (Athlete) L (Leader) T (Teammate). Captains are *SALT* of the team.

> Leaders are critical to our success for a variety of reasons. Finding and developing just one effective leader can be challenging enough for most teams. However, there should be five kinds of leaders in the program.
>
> The 5 Kinds of Leaders Every Team Needs to Be Successful include:
> 1. Performance Leaders (Competition Captains)
> 2. Locker Room Leaders (Culture Captains)
> 3. Social Leaders (Chemistry Captains)
> 4. Organizational Leaders (Campus Captains)
> 5. Reserve Leaders (Sub Captains)

Promote Academic Importance of Athletic Programs

Student-athletes are more successful than the average student. In a recent study on academic achievement, administrators reviewed results for both student athletes and their non-athlete peers (Milder, 2019). Student athletes out-performed their non-athlete peers in every subject and grade-level on the 2010 TAKS test. The benefits of athletics are numerous. Following directions from coaches translates into following directions in the classroom also. The same study showed student athletes are disciplined almost 10% less than their non-athlete peers (18.9% vs 28.4%). "We really see our program as a two-prong approach," said Stanley Laing, Northside ISD Athletic Director. "The first prong is interventions. Interventions are for the students that need more time to learn. Athletics gives these students extra support and motivation to stay in school and not drop out. The poise, character, and self-discipline that is developed in athletics enhances successful student learning in the classroom." Laing went on to discuss the second prong, which he called enrichment. "This is for the students that already 'have it'. Athletics stretches these students to go above and beyond the commitment to excellence in the spirit of competition as well as academic success." (Milder, 2019, pp. 2-3)

The facts are clear. Student-athletes have higher academic results, better attendance, and lower dropout rates than students not participating in school activities.

Improve Coaches' Abilities and Skills Through Professional Development and Continuous Improvement

Great athletic directors provide support and resources to all staff in professional development. The athletic director promotes opportunity by involving all staff in policy, procedures, and practice of the department. Through evaluation, head coaches and athletic director(s) will collaborate on the individual needs list for staff. Consideration will be given to developing a professional development plan. One size does not fit all.

Through regular assessments, using data and necessary surveys (involving stakeholders), needed professional learning will be identified. Data from these resources, plus sport related information, will help leaders understand what is needed for their individual programs.

After identifying the needs, a plan will be developed by each head coach, reviewed by the athletic director, and then implemented. All efforts will be to implement departmental growth, improve instruction, improve student-athlete performance, increase team success, and create a positive and inclusive learning environment.

It is the athletic director's job to provide flexible funding and opportunities in providing necessary educational opportunities for staff, sustain collaboration, promote mentoring, and improve production.

Engage Community Stakeholders

- Develop an Athletic Advisory Committee
- Research and utilize community members as volunteers in athletic study hall
- Have a top-down booster club: quarterly rules review, business meeting, annual goal review
- Four segments of town meetings-seminars

Facility Awareness

Athletic directors oversee directing, maintaining, and scheduling facility updates. This is a critical area and has caused many athletic directors to fail. It is a must to document every facility the athletic department uses. The diagram below is an example of full documentation: when the facility was built, and updates. It is impossible to have a good budget without having a thorough facility plan.

Example of Facility Schedule

Facility	Recommended Life Span	Installment Year	Replacement Year	Estimated Cost	Facility Built	Year for Completion	Comments	Budget
Practice Fields/ Lighting and Electrical Replacement	25 years	1999	2047	$200,000	1999	Completed 2017	Completed	Athletics
Field Turf at Main Stadium	8 years	2009	2017	$450,000-500,000	Phase 1- 2000	Summer 2017		Maint.
Tennis Court surface	7 years	2012	2019	$24,000	1999-2000	Summer 2019	If necessary	Maint.
Scoreboard Video Screen	5 years	2013	2018	$125,000	2001	Spring/Summer 2018		Maint.
Jr. High Track surface	15 Years	2014	2029	$181,963	1996	Completed 2014		Maint.
Jr. High Track surface re-spray	5 Years	2014	2019	$100,000	1996	Summer 2019	Due for Respray in 2019	Maint.
Main Stadium re-spray surface	5 years	2009	2014	$90,380	2000	Completed 2014	5 Years after next re-surface	Maint.
Main Stadium resurface	5 years	2014	2019	$100,000	2000	Summer 2019	If respray lasts 5 years	Maint.
Gym Floor strip/re-painting—Gym 1	12-15 years	2007	2019-2022	Estimate In Process	2007	Summer 2022		Maint.
Gym Floor strip/re-painting—Gym 2	12-15 years	? Approx 2002	2017	$15,000	1986	Summer 2017		Maint.
Gym Floor strip/re-painting—Jr. High Gym 1	12-15 years	? Approx 1993	2025	$14,000	1967	Completed 2015	Completed	Maint.
Gym Floor strip/re-painting—Jr. High Gym 2	12-15 years	2006	2026	$15,000	2006	Completed 2016		Maint.
Gym Floor strip/re-painting—2nd Jr. High	12-15 years	1995	2026	$14,500	1996	Completed 2016	Needs to be completed	Maint.

Example of Facility Schedule, Continued

Facility	Recommended Life Span	Installment Year	Replacement Year	Estimated Cost	Facility Built	Year for Completion	Comments	Budget
Gym Floors strip/Re-finish (Dec)	6 months	Bi-annual	Bi-annual	$11,700	N/A	Summer/Winter Annual	Budgeted Annually	Athletics
Gym Floors strip/Re-finish (July)	6 months	Bi-annual	Bi-annual	$11,700	N/A	Summer/Winter Annual	Budgeted Annually	Athletics
Scoreboard–Main Stadium	10-13 years	2001	2013	$30,000	2000	Summer 2018	Date Per Athletics	Maint.
Scoreboard–Avenue E	10-13 years	? Approx 1998	2028	$7,000	1996	Completed 2015	Completed	Athletics
Scoreboard–Jr. High	10-13 years	1988	2029	$22,000	1996	Completed 2016	Completed	Maint.
Scoreboard–Baseball	10-13 years	? 2000-2001	2028	$22,792	1994	Completed 2015	Completed	Maint.
Scoreboard–Softball	10-13 years	2000	2029	$15,000	2000	Completed 2016	Completed	Maint.
Scoreboard–2nd Jr. High Gym	15-20 years	2006	2026	$5,032	1996	2026		Athletics
Scoreboard–JHS Gym 1	15-20 years	2006	2026	$5,032	1967	Summer 2026		Athletics
Scoreboard–JHS Gym 2	15-20 years	2006	2026	$5,032	2007	Summer 2026		Athletics
Scoreboard–HS Gym 1	15-20 years	2008	2023	$28,618	2000	Summer 2023		Maint.
Scoreboard–HS Gym 2	15-20 years	2006	2026	$9,749	1985	Summer 2026		Athletics
Pole Vault Pit Refurbishment	5 years	2006	Past due 2011	$6,000		Summer 2015	Completed	Athletics
High Jump Pit Refurbishment	5 years	2006	Past due 2011	$6,000		Summer 2015	Completed	Athletics
Pole Vault Pit Refurbishment	5 years	2015	2020	$6,000		Fall 2020		Athletics
High Jump Pit Refurbishment	5 years	2015	2020	$6,000		Fall 2020		Athletics
Fence on Baseball Field	10-13 Years	2015	2028	$90,930	1994	2028	Completed	Maint.

Example of Strategic Planning

ATHLETIC FACILITY RECOMMENDATIONS (Example)

As prepared by all head coaches and athletic councils

STAFF PRIORITY-These are the first priorities by the athletic staff, listed in order of preference.

- All Weather practice field(s)-Preferably two fields
    1. Include softball in-lay of bases on west end
    2. Include baseball in-lay of bases on east end
    3. Include soccer border in-lay
- Track and Field
    1. Build 2 long jump pits (Athletics explain where to build)
- Trophy Case in new gymnasium (front foyer)
- Minor Sport Field House
    1. Include tennis, golf, wrestling, track/cross country locker rooms
    2. Include wrestling mat room designed in middle of locker facility

The following are specific improvement area suggested by each sport:

Sport Priority

- Soccer–Soccer Stadium
    1. New lights for field
    2. New section of add on bleachers—one designated home and visitor
    3. Refurbish Locker Room or rebuild
- Training Room Facility
    1. Enlarge or build Storage
    2. Include an indoor sunken whirlpool for rehab in minor sport locker facility
- Baseball
    1. Batting cages
    2. Turf the infield area
    3. Turf entire stadium
    4. Add bleachers
- Softball
    1. Batting Cages
    2. Storage Facility
    3. Turf field
- Basketball-Gym Facility
    1. Develop a maintenance schedule on nets, goals, standards
    2. Add or correct lights at JH (new) gym-too dim
- Swimming

    1. Develop a plan to build a natatorium

Strategic Planning: Pulling the Staff Together for "One Vision"

Strategic planning must involve the entire team. What is and who are the team players? All stakeholders need to be involved to ensure cooperation and unity. Before any vision can be taken forward, it must have direction. Look at your community. Is it innovative? Is it a dump? Does it have many resources or is very limited? Your dream of having new school buildings and/or football stadiums might not be feasible. Have members from the department, school administrators, and faculty as well as community people (parents, business owners, etc.) involved.

Have dreams, then plan for dreams to come true. Look at all resources and listen to opinions. In a very short time, you will see the direction of your community. In Lencioni's (2002) book, *The Five Dysfunctions of a Team: A Leadership Fable*, commitment will not come to fruition unless every suggestion is considered. The team leader must carefully facilitate brainstorming.

Work the Plan

A dream must have a plan. If the plan gets put on the shelf, then it goes nowhere. Now it is time to have a timetable and work the plan. For a plan to work efficiently, you must include the entire team. Never work the plan alone. It will fail. Include everyone, each person has a voice and a role. Decide together on individual expectations and post the action plan. Promote the decisions with local media and social media. Keep the plan visible. Show developments. Have you ever seen a fundraising campaign poster showing $0 to the desired amount? The mark gets closer and closer to the goal. This way people are a part of the goals drive.

Have a Date for Completion

Let the team be a part of determining the date.

Follow-Up on the Project

Good strategic plans have a strong push. Thorough facilitators understand a team's progress is essential to completing projects. Have feedback checks in place. Timeframes and goals must be specific. Show contributions. Have periodic check-in emails and have an open line of communication. There will be obstacles. Share these with the team.

Example of Developing an Athletic Hall of Fame

Guidelines for Nomination and Election

Purpose. The purpose of an Athletic Hall of Fame is to recognize and honor former athletes, coaches, administrators and supporters who excelled in their respective sports or coaching/support roles and helped bring recognition, distinction, and excellence by their conduct both on and off the field or court of competition. This recognition helps maintain the spirit, pride, and sense of community as well as serving as a historical account of the great traditions.

Details. A hall of fame trophy case will be placed in the lobby of the gymnasium. All recipients selected will have a gold plate placed on a plaque with their name and graduation date for the athlete, name and years of service for the coaches, administrators, or supporters, and the sports of participation.

Eligibility for Nomination. Athletes are eligible for nomination 10 years after their class graduation. They must be in good standing or in special circumstances as determined by the Board Members. Such athletes must have competed in a sanctioned varsity sport and must have excelled in such sport. Among the accomplishments considered will be individual honors (All-District, All-Area, All-State), team accomplishments, individual school or team records held, impact on teams, the overall athletic program during their era, and accomplishments thereafter.

Nomination is also open to coaches or administrators, who must have participated with distinction and/or made significant contributions to athletics, as evidenced, for example, by the success of their teams and the acknowledgement of their former student-athletes. Such coaches or administrators shall be eligible for nomination beginning 5 years after employment. Such coaches or administrators can be eligible regardless of the reason they left as determined by the Board Members.

As determined by the Board Members, contributors will also be considered for nomination based upon their service and dedication to the athletic programs.

Nomination Process. Candidates may be nominated for Hall of Fame membership by any member of the board. Formal nomination shall be made using the nomination form prescribed for such purpose and made available to the public. The nomination form must be received by the athletic department by a selected date. Application packets will be sent to the nominee by the athletic department. All applications are to remain confidential and only to be shared among the members of the Board. Information relating to a nominee's career statistics, records, achievements, etc. must be supported by accompanying documentation or sources cited so the information may be verified independently.

All application packets from the nominee must be received by the Athletic Department 1 month after selection date, to be considered for the induction into the fall class. Both the nomination form and the application packet will be available through the Athletic Department or on the web site.

Board Members

Board Members will consist of

- Director of Athletics
- Chairperson
- Associate Athletic Director
- Retired or Former Administrators (2)
- Booster Club Members (2)
- Current athletic coaches
- Retired or former athletic coach
- Current or former faculty member

Director of Athletics or designee shall appoint all Board Members.

Election Process

The Board Members shall meet at a time determined by the Chairman to nominate, review, and elect candidates. The quorum for any meeting at which election of candidates shall take place shall be a majority of the members. Background information on each nominee should be distributed to the Board Members prior to the meeting and members should familiarize themselves with the nominees prior to voting. Each Board Member shall have one vote and all votes shall carry equal weight. For election, a candidate is required to receive a number of votes equal to 75% threshold described above of those members present at the meeting. Candidates shall be discussed in alphabetical or chronological order as designated by the Chairman.

The outcome of the verbal vote will be shared with the Board Members only. If, in the opinion of the Board Members (as evidenced by failure to obtain the 75% threshold described above), no candidate nominated in a particular year is worthy of election to the Hall, so be it, it is not necessary to induct new members each year. At the same time, there shall be no limit on the number of members who may gain admission in a given year.

Induction Ceremony

The Board shall at a time and place designate an induction ceremony. However, it is commonly desired to have the induction ceremony at pre-game of a varsity football game. Inductees and their guests will be given tickets for attendance.

Fundraising: What is Fundraising? The Art of Fundraising. Different Fundraising Methods. Proper Use of Funds Raised

Fund raising is amazingly simple. It is when an organization is seeking financial support for a charity, cause, or other enterprise. There is an art to fundraising that many coaches and administrators never realize. Most people consider fundraising to be a period when an effort is made to help fund a project. In athletics, this is usually when a sport is preparing for their season. In most communities there are only so many individuals and businesses able to contribute. Every school activity, city recreational activity, and community event seeks funds from the same resources. This process of soliciting financial support to bring in revenue for an organization's mission with a clear vision. Fundraising is so much more than just asking for money. It is an opportunity to build relationships, bring in organizational support, and attract new fans and donors.

The Art of Fundraising

Are you just wanting a sponsor's money? If so, the consistent ability to fund raise will be limited. To open the doors of fundraising, make friends. How can we help the donor? How can our organization be of service to the community?

2 Corinthians 9:6-8

"Remember this: Whoever sows sparingly will also reap sparingly, and whoever sows generously will also reap generously. Each of you should give what you have decided in your heart to give, not reluctantly or under compulsion, for God loves a cheerful giver."

Have a story to tell. Have a goal. Know what your needs are and fulfilling the need will be beneficial to everyone. Donors react emotionally to inspirational stories. Donors (sponsors) do not receive a product or service like consumers. The dividend they receive is a sense of well-being. They feel good about giving and can see the need. They become a part of the organization in a way.

This is the art of fundraising. It has a premise and the donor becomes a hero to the organization. The donor feels good by helping.

The premise has a corollary: *"Donors are nourished by their kind and unselfish act of giving. This act provides satisfaction."* (David Bailiff)

How does a donor feel part of the organization? Genuinely giving time to the donor. Organizations must nurture a relationship. Provide information and updates about projects. Write thank you letters and give trinkets as a token of your appreciation. Have players write notes. Have a picture day where donors can take pictures with coaches and players. The list is endless of what you can do to nurture and build a list of loyal donors.

Potential donors are unaware of your cause. Direct mail, Facebook posts, banner ads, TV spots, radio spots and the likes do not involve donors individually. If the project is worth succeeding, then it is worth talking time to nurture a relationship, because they do not know you. See them face-to-face. Call them, visit them, but get to know them.

Example: During the school year, place game programs, brochures, and other school literature around the community—Barber shops, hair salons, banks, and doctors' waiting rooms, anywhere there is a lobby. This is a two-way benefit. Donors (sponsors) receive advertising throughout the year and your programs receive year around advertising—a win-win proposition. This shows your donors that you are giving them recognition throughout the year, not just for the project only.

Fundraising:

1. Continually search for new donors.

2. How many friends have we developed?

3. Are donors staying with us each year? (Proves we are making friends).

4. Are we continually thinking about our donors? Have we had an appreciation game or night?

Practice fundraising as a staff. Talk through situations. Give your business cards out around town. Be thankful. Regardless how hard you work at fundraising, remember it is a numbers game. Although each business and potential donor does not give to the cause, they can be become a friend. If you stay at a school long enough, the entire town will know you, your coaches, and your program.

What if a long-time supporter is having financial difficulty, will you give them an advertisement anyway? Sure. Remember *2 Corinthians 9:6-8*. *"This is real fund raising and it is an art."* (J. Welch)

Marketing

Our marketing plan includes, but is not limited to, digital marketing, print marketing, social media, television ads, and radio ads. Marketing and fundraising closely align in structure and in the overall department goals.

Marketing plans needs to reach desired audiences. What are target areas for an athletic program? Areas should include (but are not limited to) current students, alumni, and family of all athletic programs through a concentrated plan using our website, our social media pages, community and school newspapers, regional television, and local radio.

We can measure success of our plan and event through attendance figures, hits on our website and social media platforms.

Concept of a Good Marketing Plan

Creating or furthering a brand unites a regional community.

- Provides a sense of community.
- Represents something larger.
- Relates fan to the program.
- Promotes a sense of pride and dignity.
- Provides ownership and develops loyalty.
- Creates a dynamic buzz that catches lots of attention.

A marketing plan establishes a personal connection to fans. Your plan must have ways to be tailored to fans, alumni, and community.

Make the event seem like every seat is the best seat in the house. To do this, there needs to be a slogan. Use graphics and geotargeted campaigns on social media (Facebook, Twitter, and Instagram). Have banner ads for your programs and events. All school websites should have banners and links.

One recruiter website said, *"You want to play . . . We find a way."* T-shirts, bumper stickers, and other clothing items promoted this campaign.

What are your goals? Goals should include

- Attendance at home athletic events;
- Increase financial resources available to the team;
- Increase alumni support;
- Promote merchandise purchased from a local vendor;
- Have sport programs more visible around the community (consider what your community is), most communities are larger than you realize;
- Utilize athletic department website as a promotional tool;
- Develop and maintain a strong relationship with the fan base, alumni, community, and students; and
- Develop, maintain, and create a loyal fan base.

The t-shirt says it all, "2020-Shock the World."

Local college or school district example of target market:

- Students;
- Alumni-players, great teams;
- Local high schools;
- Youth teams;
- Band Day; and
- Elementary children.

Find ways to be the best:

- Entrance surveys at events.
- Mailers to the community businesses.
- Creation of a line of merchandise. Sell at all events. Make merchandise rooms available at events or trailers to sell merchandise at home games.
- Examples of Merchandise: T-shirts, hats, sweatshirts, caps, notepads, pencils, pens, trinkets, car stickers, jerseys with player names, etc.

Great marketing departments will

- Establish and maintain contacts with:
    a. TX/OK radio stations
    b. Athletic Directors and Coaches
    c. Ministers/Pastors/Youth Directors by using
        1) Mailers
        2) Telephone calls
        3) Emails
        4) Handwritten *Thank-You Cards* from coaches, players, and administrators.
        5) Invitations/tickets to live performances
        6) Autographed pictures and other merchandise
        7) Irregular personal visits
        8) Celebration Cards
            i. Successful performances
            ii. Birthdays
            iii. Anniversaries (Personal and Organization)

Guiding the Program in New Directions and Supporting ALL Sports and Athletic Staff

The athletic director must also have a finger on the pulse of the community, institution, national, and state happenings. This person is not a person that just sits and rides the train. This person is the conductor. By staying on top of what is happening, the leader can guide the department in taking steps necessary for growth. Even when downsizing must take place, a great leader will know how to move forward.

How does the athletic director do this? Communication and knowledge are vital. Study the trends and best practices. Stay up on technology. Visit with other athletic directors of similar size institutions. Have a great working relationship with the school superintendent or college president. If a school superintendent or college president does not agree with the direction of the program, then your choice as athletic director is to either change directions or change jobs. It is important to remember, the athletic director must be gifted in "teaching" their boss what the direction needs to be and have them believe they are the ones leading the ship.

An athletic director's day is full. They are met with numerous tasks and responsibilities. Their schedule is full directing or handling a variety of tasks. These tasks include interviewing prospective coaches, evaluating staff, scheduling games and buses, depositing gate receipts, developing or overseeing budgets, verifying eligibility reports, and various other details. The days are never long enough and on top of all the daily stresses of the job, they need to be innovative and move the department forward.

Gary, Tracy, Doyle, Jack

This is a daily process for athletic directors. Every year more and more must be accomplished. If teams are not doing well, this presents a problem. If a team or teams win a title, there will be problems. Bottom line, problems are attached to the position if that is your view. It is all about attitude. Athletic directors with a positive outlook on life and are highly organized seem to be best at leading and guiding people. Coach Tracy Welch, Lake Worth Athletic Director, continually says to his teams and coaches that attitude is everything.

With complicated positions comes great expectations and responsibilities. Therefore, leaders must block out time for renewal, forward thinking, team building, and have great communication skills. Beyond the long-standing basics of the position, there are new aspects that are essential for programs to thrive and survive.

These new responsibilities must be developed, and time must be found to accomplish them. The athletic director's position is one of evolution. Change is a constant. New developments will arrive; will you be ready for them? New aspects and responsibilities become a part of being an athletic director. Get prepared. That is why it is critical to understand evolution of the position and prepare to be the best.

***Foundations of Coaching* author, Jack Welch, recommends getting on a staff providing great leadership.** The way you first learn will be the foundation for your future. Learn with integrity. Learn with trust. Learn with loyalty. Learn the right ways to do things. Love your neighbor and demonstrate you are a team player.

The great Lou Holtz said it best when he said, "Do the right thing, do the best you can, and always show people you care."

REFERENCES

Angst, F. (2019). *What does an athletic director do?* https://www.thebalancecareers.com/athletic-director-job-profile-3113301

Armstrong, L. E., Johnson, E. C., Casa, D. J., Ganio, M. S., McDermott, B. P., Yamamoto, L. M., Lopez, R. M., & Emmanuel, H. (2010). The American football uniform: Uncompensable heat stress and hyperthermic exhaustion. *Journal of Athletic Training, 45*(2), 117-127. https://doi.org/10.4085/1062-6050-45.2.117

ATAVUS. (2020). *Texas tackling certification: ATAVUS is the exclusive provider of tackling certification in Texas.* https://www.atavus.com/football/thsca

BloodbornePathogenTraining.com. (2019). *About bloodborne pathogen training.* https://www.bloodbornepathogentraining.com/about-us

Civil Rights Act of 1964, Pub.L. 88-352, 78 Stat. 241 (1964).

Collins, J. (2001). *Good to great: Why some companies make the leap . . . and others don't.* HarperCollins.

Dyer, M. (2010, November). Schools develop new strategies to retain sponsors in tough economy. *High School Today*, 8-9.

Evans, D., Gillespie, L., McKamie, W. M., Krueger, M., & Mueller, L. (2019). *Texas Tort Claims Act basics.* Texas Municipal League. https://www.tml.org/DocumentCenter/View/329/Texas-Tort-Claims-Act-PDF

Family Educational Rights and Privacy Act of 1974, 20 U.S.C. § 1232g; 34 CFR Part 99. (1974).

Garini, R. B. (2014, March 25). Who is taking care of your athletes? Bangor Daily News. https://bangordailynews.com/2014/03/25/sports/who-is-taking-care-of-your-athletes/

Garland ISD. (2020). *Student handbook and code of conduct 2020-21.* https://www.garlandisd.net/file/5025?.pdf

Garner, N. (2015, February 22). *Good to great: Principles from the book which we apply in 90 digital.* https://90digital.com/blog/how-we-work/good-great-principles-book-apply-90-digital

Good to great: Why some companies make the leap . . . and others don't. (2016, February 24). In *WikiSummaries*. http://www.wikisummaries.org/wiki/Good_to_Great:_Why_Some_Companies_M

ake_the_Leap..._and_Others_Don%27t#Chapter_1:_Good_is_the_Enemy_of_Gr eat

H.B. No. 2038. (2011). *Natasha's law.* https://capitol.texas.gov/tlodocs/82R/billtext/html/HB02038F.htm

Head coach. (2020, August 13) in *Wikipedia.* https://en.wikipedia.org/wiki/Head_coach

Hester v. Canadian I.S.D., Dkt. No. 106-R1-585 (Comm'r Educ. 1985).

Jayanthi, N. A., Post, E. G., Laury, T. C., & Fabricant, P. D. (2019). Health consequences of youth sport specialization. *Journal of Athletic Training, 54*(10), 1040-1049. https://doi.org/10.4085/1062-6050-380-18

Jonas, J. (2017). *Hazing in high school athletics.* National Federation of State High School Associations. https://www.nfhs.org/articles/hazing-in-high-school-athletics/

Kunerth, J., & Balona, D-M. (2012). *FAMU death: Brutal rituals defied ban, band members say.* Orlando Sentinel. https://www.orlandosentinel.com/news/os-xpm-2012-02-05-os-famu-hazing-narrative-20120204-story.html

Lencioni, P. (2002). *The five dysfunctions of a team: A leadership fable.* Jossey-Bass.

Lesley, B. (2010). *Money does matter! Investing in Texas children and our future.* Equity Center. https://www.equitycenter.org/sites/default/files/2018-09/moneymatters.pdf

Levin, H. M. & Belfield, C. R. (2007). Educational interventions to raise high school graduation rates. In C. R. Belfield & H. M. Levin (Eds.), *The price we pay: Economic and social consequences of inadequate education* (pp. 177-199). Brookings Institution Press.

Mannie, K. (2014). Why strength training is important for all athletes. *Coach&A.D.* https://coachad.com/articles/powerline-why-strength-training-is-important-for-all-athletes/

May, D. R., Chan, A. Y. L., Hodges, T. D., & Avolio, B. J. (2003). Developing the moral component of authentic leadership. *Organizational Dynamics, 32*(3), 247–260. https://doi.org/10.1016/S0090-2616(03)00032-9

Mazerolle, S., Casa, T., & Casa, D. (2009). Heat and hydration curriculum issues: Part 2 of 4—Exercising in the heat. *Athletic Therapy Today, 14*(3), 42-47. https://doi.org/10.1123/att.14.3.42

Mazur, E. (1996). *Peer Instruction: A User's Manual* (1st ed.). Pearson.

Meglio, J. (2011). *The importance of strength training for high school athletes.* STACK. https://www.stack.com/a/the-importance-of-strength-training-for-high-school-athletes

Merriam-Webster. (n.d.). *Merriam-Webster.com dictionary.* Retrieved July 27, 2020, from https://www.merriam-webster.com/dictionary/culture

Milder, S. (2019). *The numbers don't lie: Athletics strengthens student performance and doesn't even cost that much.* Friends of Texas Public Schools. https://www.fotps.org/post/the-numbers-don-t-lie-athletics-strengthens-student-performance-and-doesn-t-even-cost-that-much

Mosher, G. (2015). *How 'culture beats scheme' becomes Eagles' motto.* Sports Philadelphia. https://www.nbcsports.com/philadelphia/philadelphia-eagles/how-culture-beats-scheme-became-eagles-motto

National Federation of State High School Associations. (2017). *Suggested guidelines for management of concussion in sports.* https://www.nfhs.org/media/1018446/suggested_guidelines__management_concussion_april_2017.pdf

National Federation of State High School Associations. (2020). *State coaching requirements: Concussion in sports.* https://nfhslearn.com/home/coaches

O'Brien, J. G. (2008). *Course Syllabus: A Learning-Centered Approach* (2nd ed.). Jossey-Bass.

Ohio University. (2020, February 6). *5 Tips for a Strong Relationship Between Coach & Athlete.* https://onlinemasters.ohio.edu/blog/5-tips-for-a-strong-relationship-between-a-coach-and-an-athlete/

Peráček, P. (2018, October 10). *Tactical Preparation in Sport Games and Motivational Teaching of Sport Games Tactics in Physical Education Lessons and Training Units | IntechOpen.* Intechopen.Com. https://www.intechopen.com/books/sport-pedagogy-recent-approach-to-technical-tactical-alphabetization/tactical-preparation-in-sport-games-and-motivational-teaching-of-sport-games-tactics-in-physical-edu

Petraglia, A., Bailes, J., & Day, A. (2015). *Handbook of neurological sports medicine: Concussion and other nervous system injuries in the athlete.* Human Kinetics.

Porter, C. (2017, February 8). *States Strive to Involve Students in Athletics Before High School.* www.nfhs.org. https://www.nfhs.org/articles/states-strive-to-involve-students-in-athletics-before-high-school/

Professionalism: Developing This Vital Characteristic. (2020). Mind Tools. https://www.mindtools.com/pages/article/professionalism.htm

Quotewise.com. (n.d.). *John Wooden quotes*. http://www.quoteswise.com/john-wooden-quotes.html

Sabock, M. D., & Sabock, R. J. (2017). *Coaching: A Realistic Perspective* (11th ed.). Rowman & Littlefield.

Simon, R. (2013). *The Ethics of Coaching Sports: Moral, Social and Legal Issues* (1st ed.). Westview Press.

Stöppler, M. C. (2020). *Hyponatremia (low blood sodium)*. https://www.medicinenet.com/hyponatremia/article.htm

Strock, J. (2018). *Serve to Lead: 21st Century Leaders Manual* (2nd ed.). CreateSpace.

Tagore, R. (n.d.). *Quotes*. https://www.brainyquote.com/quotes/rabindranath_tagore_134933

Texas Classroom Teachers Association. (1985). *"Coaching them up" contract rights*. https://tcta.org/node/13019

Texas Education Agency. (2019). *Chapter 61. School district. Subchapter EE. Commissioner's rule on reporting child abuse or neglect, including trafficking of a child*. http://ritter.tea.state.tx.us/rules/tac/chapter061/ch61ee.html

Texas Education Code. (2011). *Title 2. Public education. Subtitle G. Safe schools. Chapter 38. Health and Safety. Subchapter D. General provisions*. https://statutes.capitol.texas.gov/Docs/ED/htm/ED.38.htm

Texas Education Code. (2017a). *Title 2. Public education. Subtitle D. Educators and school employees and volunteers. Chapter 21. Educators. Subchapter A. General provisions*. https://statutes.capitol.texas.gov/Docs/ED/htm/ED.21.htm

Texas Education Code. (2017b). *Title 2. Public education. Subtitle G. Safe schools. Chapter 37. Discipline: Law and order. Subchapter A. Alternative settings for behavior management. Sec. 37.152*. https://statutes.capitol.texas.gov/Docs/ED/htm/ED.37.htm

TexasLawHelp.org. (2020). *Title IX and gender equality in Texas public school athletics*. https://texaslawhelp.org/article/title-ix-and-gender-equality-texas-public-school-athletics

Texas School Safety Center. (2020). *Texas bullying laws*. https://txssc.txstate.edu/videos/bullying-and-the-law/

Thompson, B. (2014). *Termination without tears*. https://schoolleadership.net/project/termination-without-tears/

United Nations. (1992). *What is sexual harassment*. https://www.un.org/womenwatch/osagi/pdf/whatissh.pdf

University Interscholastic League. (2012). *Concussion acknowledgement form*. https://www.uiltexas.org/files/alignments/12-13_Concussion_Acknowledment_Form1.pdf

University Interscholastic League. (2020a). *ATAVUS online procedures/directions for tackling training*. https://www.uiltexas.org/football/page/atavus-online-procedures-directions-for-tackling-training

University Interscholastic League. (2020b). *Football rules & guidelines*. https://www.uiltexas.org/football/rules-guidelines

University Interscholastic League. (2020c). *Guidelines for booster clubs*. https://www.uiltexas.org/policy/guidelines-for-booster-clubs

University Interscholastic League. (2020d). *Preparticipation physical evaluation – medical history*. https://www.uiltexas.org/files/athletics/forms/PrePhysFormRvsd1_10_20.pdf

Van Til, C. (2019). *The growing trend of sport specialization: Is it worth it?* https://www.heraldnet.com/sports/the-growing-trend-of-sport-specialization-is-it-worth-it/

Welch, J. (2012). *Coaching/teaching stipends: "Best bang for the buck."* THSCA Weekly Headlines. https://www.multibriefs.com/briefs/thsca/thsca022013.pdf

Westcott, W. L. (2012). Resistance training is medicine: Effects of strength training on health. *Current Sports Medicine Report, 11*(4), 209-216.

Wojcik, G. (2019). *Are you hydrated? Our pee color chart will tell you*. https://www.healthline.com/health/hydration-chart

DR. JACK WELCH

Dr. Jack Welch is in his second year serving as the Special Teams Coordinator, Running Backs Coach, and Football Camp Director for Texas A&M University-Commerce. In his first season with the Lions, Welch's special team units led almost every category (seven) in the Lone Star Conference with several players receiving honors. Dominique Ramsey was voted All-American/All-LSC returner. Receiving All-LSC honors were Wyatt Leah (deep snapper), Andrew Gomez (punter), and Jake Viquez (kicker). Antonio Lealiiee received first team All-LSC Running Back.

Welch has had an extensive coaching career serving both in the collegiate and high school ranks. He retired as the all-time winningest coach at Copperas Cove High School, recording a stellar 193-84-1 record in 24 years. He is in the top 100 winning head coaches in the history of Texas High School Football. He was selected as the 1998 Texas Coach of the Year. Welch led the Bulldawgs to the state playoffs 18 times, won 7 district, 10 bi-district, 5 area, 4 regional, 3 quarterfinal, and 2 state semi-final championships. During his tenure, the 'Dawgs had 15 players go to the NFL/CFL/XFL, including Heisman Trophy winner Robert Griffin III, and NFL Man of the Year Charles "Peanut" Tillman.

Welch has served as a head collegiate coach at Kansas Wesleyan University and Ft. Scott Community College. At KWU, Welch was the youngest head football coach in America at 27 years of age. He inherited the nation's longest collegiate losing streak and constructed a complete turnaround with a winning season in only his second year. At Ft. Scott Community College, he led the Greyhounds to five consecutive winning seasons, three consecutive bowl games, and a regular season conference championship.

Welch also had stints as an NCAA Division I assistant coach, serving as Offensive and Special Teams Coordinator at West Texas State and Special Teams Coordinator/Tight End Coach at Louisiana Tech.

Welch was a multi-sport collegiate letterman (football, baseball, track, and field). He is one of the all-time top 10 javelin throwers in Taylor University history. Welch led the Trojan football team his senior season in rushing and total offense. He received All-Conference honors as a fullback and was named to the TU Athletic Hall of Fame (2013). He was offered a free agency contract with the Cincinnati Bengals.

Welch was a high school multi-sport letterman receiving unanimous All-District and All-State honors at Bridgeport High School in baseball. He received a professional try-out with the Texas Rangers, making the last cut but chose to attend college. He was the runner-up Texas Champion in the light heavy weight boxing division of the Texas Golden Gloves. His junior season, he played fullback on the state champion Osawatomie, Kansas Trojan football team.

Welch received a doctorate degree from the University of Mary Hardin-Baylor (2013), master's degree from West Texas State (1983), and bachelor's degree from Taylor University (1980).

Welch is married to his high school sweetheart, Carol "Suzie" Welch, and has two sons, Josh and Steven. He has two brothers. Tracy Welch, current Athletic Director and Head Football Coach at Lake Worth High School and Gary, who served as an assistant coach (Linebackers) under Jack at both FSCC and KWU.

Seasonal History

2019-Present: Special Teams Coordinator/Running Backs–Texas A&M-Commerce

1994-2017: Athletic Director/Head Football Coach–Copperas Cove High School

1993: Special Teams Coordinator/Tight Ends–Louisiana Tech University

1987-1992: Athletic Director/Head Football Coach–Ft. Scott Community College

1985-1986: Head Football Coach–Kansas Wesleyan University

1982-1984: Offensive/Special Teams Coordinator–West Texas State University

1981 Athletic Director/Head Football Coach–Santo High School

1980: Graduate Assistant–West Texas State University

DAVID BAILIFF

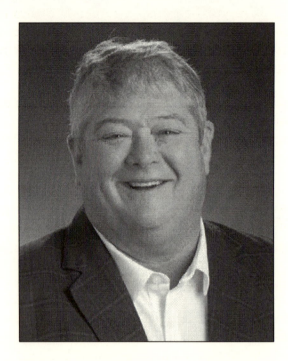

Texas A&M University-Commerce introduced David Bailiff as its 20th head football coach, on December 12, 2018, and he enters his second season as the Lions' head coach in 2020.

In the 2019 season, Bailiff led the Lions to an 11-3 record, their fifth straight NCAA Division II Championship playoff appearance, and the Super Region Four final. The Lions were ranked No. 11 nationally in the final rankings of the season by the American Football Coaches' Association.

He became the fourth-ever coach to qualify for the Division II playoffs, Division I-AA/FCS playoffs, and win a Division I-A/FBS bowl game. The 11 wins was the most ever by a Lion coach in their first season in the blue and gold.

He was the head coach for five All-American selections in his first year in Commerce, as Dominique Ramsey earned three honors and Amon Simon earned two. Simon was the Lone Star Conference Offensive Lineman of the Year. Alex Shillow was named a CoSIDA Second Team Academic All-American, Lone Star Conference, Fred Jacoby Male Academic Athlete of the Year, and LSC Football Academic Player of the Year. Shillow was also elected to a second term as the National Chair of the NCAA Division II Student-Athlete Advisory Committee.

Twenty-three Lions earned postseason honors from the Lone Star Conference in 2019, including six first team all-conference selections.

Bailiff was the head coach at Texas State University from 2004-06 and at Rice University from 2007-17. The Lions' 2019 season will be Bailiff's 15th season as a collegiate head coach.

In his tenure as a collegiate head coach, Bailiff has led a team to the NCAA Division I National Semifinals and has made five total postseason appearances with a 5-2 postseason record. The 2005 Texas State Bobcats were Division I National Semifinalists, and Bailiff led the Rice Owls to four bowls with a 3-1 record in those games.

Bailiff has led teams to 10-win seasons in three seasons (one at Texas State, two at Rice). Under his watch, the Owls had the most wins in school history over a two (18), three (25), and four (30) year periods. Rice's 18-9 mark from 2013-14 was the second-best of any FBS program in Texas.

"I am so thrilled to be the 20th head coach in the history of the school. I'm an old Lone Star Conference guy, and that's where my roots are in college football," Bailiff said. "It's great and exciting what Coach Carthel built here, and it's the first job I've had where you've got to look at the blueprint and continue building the momentum on something great he's already got started."

Bailiff was twice honored by his peers as Conference USA Coach of the Year (2008 & 2013) and led the Owls to their first outright conference championship in 56 years in 2013. His Southland Conference championship at Texas State in 2005 was the Bobcats' first conference title in their 21 years as a Division I school at the time.

While reaching new heights on the field, Bailiff's Rice teams excelled in the classroom while also making a profound impact on the Houston community. Twice in his tenure, the American Football Coaches Association honored the Owls with its Academic Achievement Award after having posted a 100% graduation rate. Rice led Conference USA football teams in GPA in seven of his first 10 seasons and annually dominated Texas on the conference in the NCAA's annual graduation rate studies.

He was honored with the Greater Houston Football Coaches Association's John Kelley Distinguished Service Award and by the Conference USA Student-Athlete Advisory Committee (SAAC) Coaches Choice Award winner for 2011-12. He was also cited by the Houston Press as "Houston's Best Sports Role Model" in its 2013 Best of Houston edition.

Rice had eight players taken in the NFL Draft during Bailiff's tenure, matching the output of the previous 22 years prior to his arrival.

In 2005 at Texas State, Bailiff was named the American Football Coaches Association's Region 5 Coach of the Year and finished third in the voting for the Eddie Robinson Award presented annually to the top coach in Division I-AA.

Prior to being named Texas State head coach, Bailiff spent three seasons on the staff at TCU. He served as the Horned Frogs' defensive coordinator in both 2002 and 2003 while working with the team's defensive linemen.

He began his coaching career as the defensive line coach at New Braunfels High School (1982-84). He went into private business from 1984-88 before returning to the coaching ranks as a defensive graduate assistant coach at Texas State in 1988. He was elevated to the Bobcats' defensive line coach in 1989.

Bailiff left Texas State in 1992 for an assistant coaching position at New Mexico. He returned to Texas State in 1997 as defensive coordinator and added assistant head coach responsibilities to his role in 1999.

In 1999, Bailiff was selected the NCAA Division I-AA Assistant Coach of the Year by the American Football Coaches Association. While at TCU, Bailiff was also honored as the Top Assistant Football Coach by the All-American Football Foundation following the Horned Frogs' 2002 season.

As a player, Bailiff was named All-Lone Star Conference as well as All-America honorable mention while playing at Southwest Texas State from 1977-80. He served as a team captain in 1980 and was named honorable mention to the Lone Star Team of the Decade.

Bailiff is married to the former Angie Daniels of Versailles, MO. He has a daughter, Brooke, and the couple has twin sons, Grayson and Gregory.

DR. JASON MAYO

Jason Mayo is a professional educator with nineteen years of experience, serving thirteen years as a campus administrator at all three levels—elementary, middle, and high school. Dr. Mayo is currently the principal at Temple High School.

Dr. Mayo has also taught at the college level since 2015. Courses include: Classroom & Behavior Management Techniques, School Law, Curriculum and Instruction, and Curriculum Design.

Dr. Mayo is married to Audrey, who is an elementary school teacher in Killeen ISD. They are the proud parents of two children, Jase and Sydney ages eleven and nine.

DR. JIMMY SHUCK

Dr. Jimmy Shuck is a professional educator with 28 years of experience. He has served as principal at elementary, junior high, alternative, and high school campuses. Dr. Shuck is currently the principal at Copperas Cove High School.

Dr. Shuck has also coached at the junior high and high school levels. As a varsity assistant coach, he has had the honor of coaching in two state championship games, four semi-final games, and six quarter final games.

Dr. Shuck is married to Rebekah, who is an elementary school principal in Copperas Cove ISD. They are the proud parents of two children, Jacob and Megan ages 27 and 22.

TRACY WELCH

Tracy Welch is a professional educator with thirty-three years of experience. He currently serves Lake Worth ISD as Athletic Director and Head Football Coach. He previously served as Associate Athletic Director, Assistant Head Football Coach, and Offensive Coordinator at Copperas Cove ISD for twenty-four years. In 2003, Tracy was named "AFLAC National Assistant Coach of the Year." He has a vast coaching background. He served as assistant offensive line coach at Kansas State University (1993 Copper Bowl Champions). He also had stints as interim athletic director and head football coach at Fort Scott Community College in spring of 1993 and Offensive Coordinator from 1988-1992. He was instrumental in producing three consecutive bowl appearances, a conference championship, and five consecutive nationally ranked offenses.

In addition, Tracy served six years as a head high school track coach. His track teams finished as district runner-up and district champions four respective years. He had three regional runner-up championships and a third place State 5A finish, with his 4x100 meter relay team having the fourth best time in the nation.

He is married to Sheri, who is an administrator in Azle ISD. They are the proud parents of three children, Kaylee (20), and two sons, Caleb (17) and Matthew (15).

Made in the USA
Coppell, TX
05 October 2020